D1481954

A Behavioral Study of
Rural Modernization

Charles A. Murray

foreword by
Lucian W. Pye

The Praeger Special Studies program—utilizing the most modern and efficient book production techniques and a selective worldwide distribution network—makes available to the academic, government, and business communities significant, timely research in U.S. and international economic, social, and political development.

A Behavioral Study of Rural Modernization

Social and Economic Change in Thai Villages

PRAEGER SPECIAL STUDIES IN INTERNATIONAL ECONOMICS AND DEVELOPMENT

Praeger Publishers   New York   London

Library of Congress Cataloging in Publication Data

Murray, Charles A
    A behavioral study of rural modernization.

    (Praeger special studies in international economics
and development)
    Bibliography: p.
    1. Rural development--Thailand.   2.   Thailand--Rural
conditions.   3.   Villages--Thailand.   I.   Title.
HN700.55.A8M87   1977   309.2'63'09593   77-7827
ISBN 0-03-022856-5

PRAEGER SPECIAL STUDIES
200 Park Avenue, New York, N.Y., 10017, U.S.A.

Published in the United States of America in 1977
by Praeger Publishers,
A Division of Holt, Rinehart and Winston, CBS, Inc.

789   038   987654321

Printed in the United States of America

For Alan and Frances Murray

Applying a very sophisticated and ingenious technique of analysis, Charles A. Murray has found a new approach to solving what some have judged to be the hardest problem in understanding "modernization" and social change. Simply stated, this knotty problem, first explored by Durkheim and Marx, is "Why is it that modernization produces a vibrant dynamic, optimistic society in some cases, while in others demoralization, social degeneration and anomie are the result?"

In recent years this fundamental question has reappeared in numerous guises. Leaders of less developed countries have been perplexed as to whether their people should turn their backs on ancient traditions and strive to become "new men," or whether the road to modernization requires that they rediscover the roots of their collective, historic identity. Intellectuals recognize an unresolved dilemma. Isn't it necessary for a society to cast aside many of its old habits and values in order to modernize? Yet, is it not also true that any society which forgets its traditional values is certain to become less human and incapable of supporting the good life which modernization supposedly promises?

After observing conditions in Thailand for many years, D. Charles Murray decided to find out, as scientifically as possible, why the spread of modernization made some villages obviously happy, prosperous, and progressive places, while others became demoralized, strife-ridden, and stagnating places. He noted that outside assistance could readily generate further progress in the "healthy" villages, but that little could be done to help the second type.

With great skill Dr. Murray developed scales for measuring both "economic development" and the "quality of life," and then, through a complex causal modelling method, he related types of villages to indices of the readiness of villagers to engage in "personal" as contrasted with "civic" investments.

Dr. Murray discovered that there is a very important place for "traditional" values in the modernization process. Indeed, modernization without traditional values may be impossible. His findings have great consequences for all who are striving to bring about rural development in the Third World. He has made a major contribution to both our theoretical understanding of development and the application of advanced statistical techniques to behavioral studies of modernization.

PREFACE

This study is an attempt to answer a question that I formed over a period of six years spent in Thailand. Its exact expression varied with my preoccupations. At the outset I was a Peace Corps Volunteer, and the question was the very practical one facing development workers in the field: Why is it so much easier to get things done in one village than in another just down the road? Some villages were "good" villages, and some were "bad"; everybody in the district office knew which were which; but nobody could pin down exactly what it was about the villages that made the difference.

A few years later, I was conducting research into the responses of villagers to local development inputs, and for the first time got a look at the interior business of a village, which is so easily disregarded by the development worker. It clearly played a large part in the villager's life and had very little relationship to anything that the central government did or failed to do. The question at that point was where some of the impressive administrative capabilities of villages had originated, and why they were so much better utilized in some villages than in others.

A year later, the insurgency was occupying my attention. Driving through what were euphemistically called "sensitive" areas, I would be told that the village we were passing had sent 20 of its sons to join the insurgent bands. A few minutes later I would be told that the next village had sent no one, and in fact had rejected numerous recruiting efforts. Why such different responses? None of the standard answers was good enough.

After a hiatus for graduate work, I returned to Thailand to participate in a project being conducted by the American Institutes for Research for the United States Agency for International Development, dealing with the problem of assessing the impact of development at the local level. The data that responded to the immediate demands of that project also permitted me to investigate the general questions I had been circling: Why do villages react so differently to the problems of modernization, and what is the nature of the difference? This book is the result.

At the bottom, all of the formulations of the question are different approaches to the underlying issue of quality of life in a village, and the reasons why it can vary so widely in communities of roughly equal wealth, size, and accessibility. Strictly speaking, it is still a nearly unresearchable topic. Quality of life as a variable in the social sciences is exceedingly elusive, most of all when it is applied to an alien culture. But even if the book contains no construct explicitly labeled "quality of life," it was motivated by the notion that villages are different, in ways that are at the heart of the happiness and well-being of at least those three out of four Thai who still live in villages—and perhaps villagers elsewhere as well.

I have space to mention only a few of the many people who have contributed to the development of this book. At the American Institutes for Research, Robert E. Krug, director of the Thailand project during my field work, deserves special thanks for his patience while I struggled through the initial formulation of the argument. My thanks also go to three officials of the Agency for Accelerated Rural Development who assisted during the field work— Suthat Khlangsuphan, Chaiyasit Hotorakit, and Sivasak Seubsaeng—and to that agency and the United States Agency for International Development for permission to apply the data from the Thailand project to these additional analyses.

At the Massachusetts Institute of Technology, Lucian W. Pye, Ithiel de Sola Pool, and Douglas A. Hibbs each played a key role throughout my graduate work and were of particular help in shaping this study. John D. Montgomery very generously let me borrow from his original investment construct and gave me the right push as the right moment to reach closure on the study. Eugene Webb was a source of advice at critical moments and my inspiration for seeking unobtrusive measures.

Above all, three persons have been instrumental. One is Pholachart Kraiboon, friend and colleague in the 41 villages of this study and perhaps a hundred others over the years. The second is Paul A. Schwarz, who has been teacher and critic on this as on so many of my efforts since 1969. The third is Suchart Mrrray, my wife, who in addition to translating and annotating a mountain of field interviews served as resident expert on what the Thai really think.

CONTENTS

LIST OF TABLES AND FIGURES

A Behavioral Study of
Rural Modernization

A VILLAGE PERSPECTIVE
ON MODERNIZATION

Most of our strategies for promoting modernization in peasant societies assume that quality of life in traditional villages goes up as villagers increase their income and have greater accessibility to the institutions and services of a modern outside world. A main obstacle to achieving these changes is often taken to be the peasant himself, who, it is felt, is too conservative, too poor, or too confused to adopt the required innovations.

This study explores an alternative approach: that while economic modernization can bring with it significant advantages to the individual, it also tends to degrade the quality of community life on equally significant dimensions. The dimensions in question are not quaint, or romantic, or even inherently "traditional" as opposed to "modern." They are norms of social and political interaction that comprise the rules for getting along with neighbors, settling disputes, solving problems, and protecting the family.

That modernization acts against these norms is the first half of the argument. The other half is that they are worth protecting. The affective reasons for that assertion will not be argued at length; only enough to indicate that the norms in Thailand are as plausibly civilized as any substitute we in the West have to offer as a replacement. The central part of the justification for protecting and nourishing them is that, given their survival, the village has a potential for coping with the dislocations of modernization that has gone largely unrecognized and is in danger of being lost altogether.

THE VILLAGE AS THE UNIT OF ANALYSIS

Thai villages differ, as any villager will confirm. Some are tranquil; some have a history of feuds. Some are pious and sober; others have a jug of moonshine

under every porch and card games every night. Some villages are proud of themselves and proclaim that they grow the sweetest tamarind or the biggest durian
or the most beautiful women in the country. Other villages are a collection of
houses with only a name for a common bond. Some villages are clean, others
are dirty. Some are spread out over several kilometers, each house hidden from
its neighbors. In others, the houses will be crammed together until their porches
touch.

Some villages are irrepressibly curious. If a stranger strolls through them,
he will be asked at every second house to stop and chat. In another village just
down the road, he can walk for an hour with hardly a greeting. If he stays for a
few days, some villages will prove to be ceremonious in their treatment of him,
others relaxed and unbuttoned, still others suspicious and aloof.

Villages are unpredictable. In one village located a few minutes away from
a large town, the visitor still has to explain that the world is round; in another,
hours from anywhere, the headman will let him listen to a recording of a Mozart
quintet, played on a wind-up Victrola.

Most importantly, some villages seem able to solve their problems while
others cannot. Some villages are victimized by conmen, their daughters seduced
by recruiters from the city's brothels, plagued by police looking for a rake-off,
unable to stop the river from flooding the fields every year—while other villages
ignore the conmen, keep out the recruiters, get the district office to rein in the
police, and build an earthen dam to hold back the river. More generally, as we
shall attempt to describe in the course of this book, some villages seem able to
ride with the punch of modernization while others cannot.

All of these are everyday aspects of life and together they shape the
quality of life in the village. There are limits, of course. An impoverished village
living on the edge of starvation is an unpleasant place to live regardless of any
other conditions. But given a typical (for Thailand) level of natural resources,
the nature of the village—its gestalt—is a crucial factor in determining whether
its inhabitants' daily existence is generally a pleasant one.

The importance of the internal strengths or weaknesses of the village is
perhaps the most commonly overlooked fact of life in developing countries.
Circumstances conspire to put competing factors in the foreground.

The administrator of rural development efforts offers an example. In the
field, the only occasion he has to visit villages is when a project is being planned,
implemented, or inspected. Unless he makes a deliberate effort to break the
pattern, he can spend years at his job and talk to hundreds of villagers and
almost never hear them discussing anything except topics related to development
projects—because development projects are what is happening in every village he
visits. If he is an administrator in the provincial office or in Bangkok, he is sur-
rounded by the plans and budgets for thousands of projects totaling millions of
dollars. It is hardly surprising that he tends to differentiate among villages in
terms of development projects and assume that they shape much of the village

life. Yet consider: the average village of the 41 in this study had been involved in less than four projects of any kind during the five years 1972-77—and that figure includes shallow-well projects that were finished in perhaps two days of labor and agriculture projects that affected only a few members of the village. It includes the failures, and the projects with only trivial effects. The aggregate figures in Bangkok are impressive, but they obscure how small a part development inputs play in the everyday life of a villager.

A parallel kind of foreshortening phenomenon afflicts the administrator in other government bureaus. When he visits a district office, he sees lines of villagers waiting to talk to officials. When a report comes to his attention about the quality of local government, it usually deals with a conspicuous case—a corrupt official who swindled a villager, or (at the opposite extreme) an official who became a minor hero by taking a sick village child to the health center. Particularly in a country with an insurgency problem, there is a tendency to assume that villager interactions with officials are a powerful determinant of the villager's attitude toward the government. Yet again consider: in three villages for which extensive data on this topic were obtained, only 39 percent of the heads of household had experienced any contact with a district official during the year before the interview, save for sitting in an audience when an official spoke to a village meeting. When it is further remembered that a head of household (a male adult in almost all cases) is likely to be the only person in the family who transacted business with the government, the presumptive proportion of village adults who had any contact with an official is smaller yet. And added to that, the year's interactions for the 39 percent were not extensive. Most often, they consisted of a single event, taking a morning's time, of entirely prosaic content. So even if occasionally the very abrasive official can cause a lasting grudge or the very helpful official can inspire good feeling, the chief characteristics of villager interaction with the government are rarity, brevity, and uneventfulness—if by government is meant the career civil servants of the Thai government.

It is understandable why development officials and civil administrators become so preoccupied with their inputs that they overlook how tiny a proportion of the village's life is involved. It is somewhat less obvious why the village as a unit of analysis has been used so seldom by scholars.

Villagers—or peasants—have not been ignored. Their role as a source of political instability and pressure for reform has been a major topic since the advent of political development as a distinct branch of political science. The "revolution of rising expectations," mobilization of new groups into the political system, the breakdown of strict social hierarchies, the modernizing effects of mass media—these and a variety of other topics have relied upon analyses of villager responses as a major component.

Nor has the "village" as archetype been ignored. The participant observation case study of a single village has been the mainstay of a major school of anthropology whereby the principal features of a culture are induced from the careful study of a representative case.

But despite the extensive attention given to the individuals who live in villages, and the microscopically detailed examination of a few archetypical villages, the treatment of villages as the unit of analysis has been highly restricted. To a surprising degree, the tacit assumption of scholarship in political development has been that one village is much like the next, with little to offer as a source of variance. This study works from the opposite viewpoint.

THE DEPENDENT VARIABLES

The unit of analysis is the village. There are two dependent variables: how much modernization has occurred among the inhabitants of a village, and how well the village is coping with it. Each measure is expressed in the form of an index combining several indicators—the Personal Investment Index for expressing individual modernization, and the Civic Investment Index for expressing the extent to which the village is coping. The content and the analysis of these indexes and the factors that impinge on them comprise the rest of the book. But it is important at the outset to state explicitly the nature of the distinction between "how much" and "how well," and why they need to be distinguished at all.

"How Much" in Rural Modernization

The question of how much personal modernization has occurred is far from new to this study. A number of attempts to instrument "personal modernity" can be found in the literature. The job has not been a simple one. Two specialists who reviewed the existing measures reached the conclusion that "At best, the *concept* of individual modernity may be meaningful as a distinct variable, but the *measurement* of modernity has apparently been unsuccessful. At worst, the notion of individual modernity as a distinct set of orientations may be a myth."* The main problem, as they saw it, was that the indicators

---

*Michael Armer and Allan Schnaiberg, "Measuring Individual Modernity: A Near Myth," *American Sociological Review* 37 (1972): 315. The four indexes of personal modernity that Armer and Schnaiberg examined are David H. Smith and Alex Inkeles, "The OM Scale: A Comparative Socio-Psychological Measure of Individual Modernity," *Sociometry* 29: 353–77; Joseph A. Kahl, *The Measurement of Modernism: A Study of Values in Brazil and Mexico* (Austin: University of Texas Press, 1968); Schnaiberg, "Rural-Urban Residence and Modernism: A Study of Ankara Province, Turkey," *Demography* 7 (1970): 71–85; and Armer, "Formal Education and Psychological Malaise in an African Society," *Sociology of Education* 43 (1970): 143–58.

used in the indexes of modernity had generally been as highly correlated with measures of anomie or socioeconomic status as with the other presumptive indicators of modernity—that is, the measures of modernity failed tests of statistical distinctiveness.

From the perspective of this study, the problem has been a very different one: The existing indexes have counted behaviors that depend on technological modernity—radio listening, movie attendance, newspaper reading, purchase of manufactured goods, and the like—without specifying exactly what it was about an indicator that reflected modernity. Substantive distinctiveness of an index is essential, whereby a conceptual basis exists for choosing among the hundreds of indicators of "degree of modernity" that might have prima facie plausibility.

In defining the nature of this substantive distinctiveness, our ambitions have been sharply restricted. No attempt has been made to develop a global definition of modernity in humans. We focus on the transitional state, the threshold, between traditional and modern. Even more specifically, we focus on the transitional state as it relates to peasants, not to all classes and occupations in traditional society. The task as it has been delimited here is to determine the essential qualitative differences between the states of "being modern" and "being traditional" for a villager, and to develop a rationale for assessing how the attitudinal transformation begins to surface in behavior.

In doing so, we share the tacit assumption of most observers that personal modernity is going to happen everywhere and regardless, sooner or later. There is also a tacit assumption (occasionally with qualms) that the interior changes in the individual are fundamentally liberating and desirable. But we stop short of accepting the inevitability or desirability of all the changes that go with personal modernity. The modernization of the economic and social landscape can take place in a variety of ways, with a variety of consequences. And that is the source of the requirement for specifying a dependent variable for measuring not only how much a community is modernizing, but also how well it is modernizing.

"How Well" in Rural Modernization

Defining "well" is the problem, and it has no unique solution. It is argued widely that there is no easy way to make the transition, and that it is best to do it rapidly and thoroughly—roughly if necessary. The disruptions that are caused are all the more acceptable if the traditional society is seen as oppressive and corrupt. At the end of the process is a net gain for the population that went through it.

This study takes an explicitly conservative, evolutionary approach. "How well" is not measured in terms of progress toward the development of liberal democracy, or Maoist communism, or any other political system that is said to stand at the end of the development process. The subject is not the political destination of traditional villages, but the journey. The terms of the question are: At any given point in the process, how well is the village governing its affairs?

This perspective is in part a function of personal predilections that are beyond defending. Having spent a number of years in and around Thai villages, the author concluded that Thai villages are essentially healthy, civilized social organizations. The changes that modernization will bring are not so urgently required, nor are the virtues of the Thai village so trivial that severe dislocations in the village should be accepted lightly. Others, including a number of Thai insurgents, profoundly disagree.

There is, however, another and less personal argument for taking an evolutionary approach to rural modernization. It grows from the difference between national modernization and modernization in the village. The latter is not the former writ small. Village modernization is a simpler, more straightforward process, in ways that bear directly on the analysis.

National governments have the freedom and the obligation to set policy and to allocate resources among priorities. Because of this, it is often inappropriate to speak of a government "coping with modernization." When a central government copes with problems raised by modernization, it is in some part dealing with the consequences of its own policy decisions. Big problems might be the calculated costs of big changes that the government felt compelled to set in motion. An outward lack of dislocating problems might be a reflection of inertia. It becomes nearly impossible to separate out the effects of wisdom (or lack of it) in the government's policy choices and the competence or incompetence it brings to administering the problems of modernization that would occur no matter what policy was pursued.

The same condition does not exist for villages, and in this lies the appropriateness of translating "coping with modernization" into operational terms. For the village, there is no problem of choice between industrial versus agricultural development, no options of social reorganization or political reform. The village exists with whatever human and natural resources it possesses, the wisdom endowed by its culture, and some resources handed down from the central government. It can only marginally alter these assets; for practical purposes over the short run, they are fixed. Moreover, they are quite limited. By no stretch of the imagination does even the wealthiest Thai village dispose of enough resources to speak meaningfully about allocation among priorities. The village has to take modernization as it comes, reacting to new situations as best it can. The village cannot plan its rate of change or type of change except within the narrowest of limits. It thus becomes reasonable to ask of a village if it is continuing to function in certain basic areas of village governance—maintenance of peace and order, sponsorship of a few simple public goods—that have profound effects on the daily life of the villager. For this study, the continued ability to perform these functions equitably and efficiently in the face of new demands and problems is argued to be a meaningful indicator of "well" in rural modernization.

CHAPTER

2

A BEHAVIORAL MEASURE
OF MODERNITY:
PERSONAL INVESTMENT

The existence of a qualitative difference between the states of "being modern" and "being traditional" has been widely recognized even while the dimensions of the difference have been at issue. Most students of the subject, whatever their perspectives, share the sentiment behind Daniel Lerner's early formulation that modernization has "some distinctive *quality* of its own, which explains why modernity is left as a *consistent whole* among people who live by its rules."[1] At the extremes—the Bangkok university student and the peasant in a remote village, for example—the difference is palpable.

But we are not dealing with the extremes. We intend to explore what happens at the changeover, the threshold—that point beyond which a person can no longer be called traditional, even if he or she is not yet modern. To do that, it is necessary to distinguish the rules of modernity from its accouterments, for modern people act in a variety of technologically modern ways that continue to expand long after personal modernity has been reached. They live in urban environments, use energy at vastly increased levels, and communicate, or are communicated with, via the press and the electronic media. But these kinds of behaviors do not necessarily reflect the bedrock "distinctive quality" that defines people as being modern. They are correlates, of most use when the subject is the modernity of technologies, not cultures; in urban centers, not villages; and the *extent* of modernity, not its threshold. We are asking: Given two villages at different points on the road between tradition and modernity, what changes in behavior in populations of those villages will allow us to identify which village is where? Determining a believable answer is essential to asking the next questions about what modernity does to and for the village.

THE TRADITIONAL OUTLOOK:
DELIMITED ASPIRATIONS

The essentials of modernity in the village are seen more easily against the backdrop of the essentials of "being traditional." For, despite the heterogeneity of village societies in Asia, Africa, Europe, and the Americas, a few common elements stand out. They are not arcane. They do not develop from obscure cultural kinships among peasants the world over. They simply make sense as the common reactions of reasonable people assessing conditions around them.

One of the common elements that has emerged is that peasants are characterized by delimited aspirations. They define "success" in terms of meeting an attainable standard, and the limits of that standard do not expand over time. What was success for grandfather and father is success for son and grandson as well.

Exceptions to the proposition exist, obviously. Every village society has had its Dick Whittingtons; many have had an occasional peasant-born emperor or minister of state. And to villagers in all peasant societies must come occasional fantasies of wealth, or at least thoughts of being something other than a poor farmer. But in terms of everyday, actionable aspirations, it appears to be a modal value of peasants to have clear bounds for themselves and their children. And it is entirely reasonable that this should be so, by the nature of the resources and the opportunities available to villagers.

In most parts of the world, being a villager means living on the margins of subsistence. There is barely enough to go around in a good year. There is the constant threat of a bad year in which there will not be enough to go around. Good year or bad there will be a steady drain on the villager's production by landlords, the state, or both. In this context, open-ended aspirations are unrealistic. The wherewithal for breaking free of the constraints in the environment is not available. On the contrary, any attempt to do so is likely to infringe on the very limited resources of a neighbor. A typical result, not suprisingly, is the development of strong social pressures to maintain the status quo on a variety of dimensions, lest attempts at personal improvements by one member of the community lead to new deficits for the others. This is the most economical explanation for the stinginess and suspicion that have been found to characterize so many peasant societies, captured most succinctly by anthropologist George Foster through his construct of the "image of limited good." The peasant sees all good things perpetually in a state of short supply, and there is nothing he can do to increase the quantities. The behavior that results from this attitude, Foster points out, "is not only highly rational in the context of the cognition that determines it, but that for the maintenance of peasant society in its classic form, it is indispensable."[2]

Delimited aspirations are not unique to villagers who people scarcity environments. Thailand is a case in point, as we discuss in more detail in Chapter 4.[3] Some goods have not been limited in traditional Thailand, nor have villagers been bound into an immobile social system. Nonetheless, the traditional Thai peasant has behaved as if goods were limited. That is, he has persistently ignored opportunities to expand his agricultural output even though he could do so without new technology and with very little capital.*

There exist numerous explanations for the "unnecessarily" delimited aspirations of the traditional Thai peasant. The proposition here, as in the case of the peasant in a scarcity environment, is that the behavior can be seen as part of a rational calculation by the peasant: this time, that the marginal short-run returns from increased production would not be commensurate with the extra work.

This is an explanation often given directly by villagers. In one isolated Northeastern village that was part of this study, for example, a cotton-growing project was a success during its first year—the crop was large and the market price was good—but was nevertheless discontinued by most of the villagers the next year. Asked why they had given up an apparently good thing, villagers explained that the cotton had been grown only because of a poor rice-growing season the previous year. In view of the improving rice production since then, villagers saw no reason to continue what had been to them an "insurance" effort with the cotton. In contrast was another village that was becoming very active in cash crop farming. The headman was asked what villagers did during the dry season. These days, he replied, almost everyone had small vegetable gardens that provided extra income. This was new, he continued: "In the old days, everyone was idle during the dry season. We could get everything we wanted from the forest. But now there are so many things to buy in the stores, everybody wants income."

This is at least partially a case of rising consumer demand of the type familiar throughout the world. The availability of goods tends to create demands for those goods. To this extent, the attempts to increase income may be caused simply by greater knowledge about the goods that money can buy. But in another sense, the nature of the goods to be bought has changed even more. What, after all, could a villager in traditional Thailand buy with extra income? Granted that the very rich lived differently from the poor, the merely "well-off" villager did not live much more comfortably than his subsistence-level neighbor;

---

*Historically, the available land in Thailand has not been filled by farmers expanding their holdings but in response to the needs of an expanding population. Even today, it is hard to find large landholders outside the Central Plains. In the 41 villages of this study, for example, the largest landholding was only 120 acres (300 rai). The next largest was only half of that.

a slightly larger house, a few more pieces of furniture, a very few store-bought items—it came to that. Small increments in income did not substantially change his life-style, and they were not needed to fill out his requirements for subsistence. Now, a few thousand extra baht of income will buy a motorcycle, a few hundred baht will buy a radio, and even five or six baht will buy a movie ticket at the district town—all of which are the kinds of purchases that do significantly alter life-style. Given this perspective, the same villager who rationally chose not to increase his production some years ago—or today, in a very isolated village— can just as rationally choose to increase under the changed circumstances.

THE MODERN TRANSITION: ACCULTURATION TO CHANGE

Unleashing one's standard of the attainable is a necessary but not sufficient condition for leaving behind the traditional outlook. Malcolm Quint's description of the idea of progress in an Iraqi village vividly conveys this limitation:[4]

> Late at night, as a group of us would sit around a dung fire, sipping tiny glasses of sweet tea, the more vocal of village elders would go off into long descriptions of the shining future. They spun dreams of the day when they would have their own land to cultivate with tractors; when the backbreaking labor involved in digging the yearly irrigation ditches and building temporary dams would be taken over by a benificent government; when they would have medical facilities in the village, or at least in the district; when they would all have radios; and so on. . . . *The fulfillment of this dream is something for which they must be patient. They know that it will be fulfilled some day in the natural course of events. They have no doubt of this; the only question is when.*

These villagers are far from being modern despite their new aspirations. Their stance toward the newly perceived goods of modernity is a cargo cult mentality, entirely passive. To be modern it is necessary not only to have an expanding standard of the attainable, but also to be comfortable in manipulating change to attain the new ends.

This criterion of modernity is embedded in the meaning of the word. If nothing else, modernization must inescapably include change as one of its components. When the issue is personal modernity, "success" must centrally mean an understanding of and ability to use the mechanisms of change. Lacking this, the new aspirations are a danger. What works for improving the life of one villager may not work for his neighbor; a crop that would grow in one village's fields may not be right for the village down the road. The trick in being modern is to learn how change works, and when, and for what.

This approach to modernization has increasingly become an informal common point of departure among the major theorists, as they try to pin down what is essential to the process of personal modernization. Frederick Frey for one has discussed his sense that seemingly different paradigms of modernization are all getting at the same thing and concludes that, at bottom, "the cardinal feature of personal modernity lies in one's attitude toward change."[5] Daniel Lerner's description of the mobile personality is a profile of the personal qualities that dispose one toward the absorption of change—a personality "distinguished by a high capacity for identification with new aspects of [the] environment."[6] Samuel Huntington paraphrases Lerner when he sets out to identify the psychological dimension of modernization.[7] David Apter focuses on the modernity of cultures rather than of men, but the tenor of his argument is familiar when he asserts that "to be modern means to see life as alternatives, preferences, choices"—that is, among other things, to initiate and manage change.[8] Everett Hagen's descriptions of high need achievement, need autonomy, and need order as they relate to economic development, all are said to center on the nature of the individual's response to flux, to change.[9] And finally, Leonard Binder, in his thoughtful introduction to the study of crises in political development, put the same theme in a philosophical perspective. It is worth quoting at some length:[10]

> For nearly ten generations Western man has been concerned with understanding and controlling the changing of his condition and circumstances. That the occurrence of change should require any special understanding is not immediately self-evident. . . . Continuity and stability are ancient desiderata whose worth must depend upon the comprehension if not the experience of change. . . . What does appear to be significant even if in no measurable sense, are two characteristics of modern Western man's intuition of the expansion and acceleration of history. The first of these is awareness of the length of the epoch of change, and the second is the prevalent, but by no means universal, favor with which change is anticipated if not experienced.

In sum, there has been a widespread recognition in the literature that acculturation to change is a hallmark, perhaps the hallmark, of modernity in men. Regardless of the features of a culture that may ease the transition to modernity, its population must make the same fundamental reorientation that has been required everywhere by the nature of the transition: the acceptance of the possibility and the desirability of utilizing change.

THE BEHAVIORAL MEASURE

The purpose of the discussion has been to identify what men do differently once they begin the transition from a traditional to a modern outlook. What are the protomodern behaviors to look for and measure?

The discussion has suggested that two criteria must be met. First, the behavior must be one that implies expanding aspirations. Second, the behavior must be one that exhibits the expectation that change is manageable and generally beneficial. Together, these criteria lead to the following proposition: Personal modernity begins for a villager when he first seeks to improve his life by voluntarily risking what he already possesses—or, as the title of the chapter indicates, modernity begins when a villager starts to invest. Expanding aspirations are implicit in the effort to seek a profit. The underlying assumption that change is manageable is implicit in the willingness to risk. Given these stances, emerging in behavior, it is also a proposition of this approach that the more complex trappings of modernity—mass media participation, preference for urban life, political mobilization, changes in family role structure, and the rest—can be ignored for certain important purposes when the topic is rural modernization. Indeed, it is argued that in the rural context they tend to be deceptive, to obscure central questions of where the village population stands relative to economic development and to social and political expectations.

Investment is formally defined as the voluntary risk of energy, money, or other physical resources in the expectation of a future return in excess of the expenditure. On the basis of the theoretical considerations that have been discussed, it is postulated that the degree of change from a traditional to a modern outlook in a set of villages can be compared by the levels of investment behavior that are taking place among their inhabitants.* The operational expression of this is a Personal Investment Index, comprised of a village's summed standardized scores on a set of behavioral indicators.

---

*There is a close kinship between "personal investment" as used here and David C. McClelland's "*n* Achievement," which measures the psychological need to achieve and which has been used by McClelland as an explanatory variable for economic growth.[11] Personal investment could be seen as a behavioral manifestation of high *n* Achievement in the context of peasant societies. But the work on *n* Achievement is associated with extensive collateral argumentation about the foundations of the achievement motive, which the personal investment construct does not try to carry. With regard to peasants, we share Foster's view: "change cognitive orientation through changing access to opportunity, and the peasant will do very well indeed; and his *n* Achievement will take care of itself."[12]

The question of whether a given behavior belongs in an investment index was decided on the basis of four culling rules. The first three are based on the content of the investment notion:

The behavior must be voluntary. Planting rice in hopes of a harvest is an investment, but what might best be called a "constrained investment" if the rice is being planted as the subsistence staple for the family. Unless the villager *chooses* to risk his resources, no modernizing content to his behavior should be inferred.

The behavior must entail risk. Putting money in a guaranteed savings account is not an investment by our definition. However, it should be noted that the risk need not involve only money. As stated in the definition, a risk of time or energy is equally suitable.

The anticipated return must be in the form of a profit, another way of saying that a purchase is not an investment. When a villager buys a tin of sardines, or even something as laden with modernizing connotations as a radio, he is presumed to be making the same informal calculations that he uses for buying a rattan fish trap. The technological novelty of the item being purchased does not in itself confer any modernizing significance to the act.

There is no stipulation that an investment behavior is inherently economic. Sending a child to study in secondary school at the province town is an investment whether or not the parents expect an eventual economic return. Complaining to the police about a grievance can be an investment, as can the act of joining a political party or the insurgents. But it happens that a villager in Thailand (and in most developing countries) has opportunities to make a variety of sound economic investments while he still has only obscure opportunities to make "sound" social and political ones. Thus most of the indicators initially available for consideration were economic ones. The decisive factor, however, in choosing among behaviors that met the first three criteria was the fourth culling rule:

The sources of epistemic error in the observations must be random. The first three rules attempted to minimize what is called epistemic error—that is, minimize the gap between the *concept* of investment and the concrete events that are to be used to reify it. But errors will remain nonetheless. The fourth culling rule stipulates that they be random. Suppose, for example, that out of 100 observations of rice mill ownership, 15 would not be interpreted as examples of investment if we could somehow penetrate into the motivations of the owners. The fourth culling rule asks that the reasons for the 15 errors be different ones or, practically speaking, as unrelated as possible.

Six potential indicators that had survived the first three criteria failed this one. The use of commercial fertilizer, improved rice seed, or insecticide is common in Thai villages, but the use of any of these items could not be included as an indicator because in some villages of the sample they were being distributed by the government at very low or now cost. In other villages, they had to be purchased. The sale of rice was also rejected as an indicator. It can denote a personal investment if the villager has deliberately planted more than his family can eat or store for future consumption; but in many cases it is a purely traditional behavior in which the sale is the incidental result of a good harvest. Two others, taking produce to sell in markets outside the village and sending children to secondary school, were eliminated because they were no-cost behaviors for people living in villages very close to the district town. A seventh indicator—ownership of a vehicle for commercial use—was delimited. Motorscooters and motorcycles serve multiple functions. The indicator was therefore restricted to four-wheeled vehicles, which are used for investment purposes virtually without exception.

Other candidate indicators (such as planting two crops a year and rental of agricultural equipment) were eliminated for lack of variance. In all, six candidate indicators met all four criteria and showed variance among the 41 villages of the sample. The six were (1) percentage of households cultivating a cash crop during the year preceding the research, (2) number of commercial vehicles per hundred households, (3) number of rice mills per hundred households, (4) number of stores per hundred households, (5) percentage of villagers in nonagricultural employment, and (6) membership in agricultural credit cooperatives.

The elements of voluntarism, risk, and profit incentive are clearcut in all cases but nonagricultural employment, which does not in itself represent risk or the expenditure of resources.* But it does reflect investment in terms of earlier decisions to acquire a skill, to edge away from a subsistence view of economics, and to be prepared to tolerate the prospect of unemployment.

Variance on all six indicators was substantial. The range of that variance is reported in Table 2.1 in terms of the mean, standard deviation, high score, and low score for each indicator.

The aggregate Index scores showed similarly broad variation. The distribution of mean scores is shown in Figure 2.1. For interpretive purposes, remember that these represent the average standardized score on the six indicators.[13]

The intercorrelations among the items in the Personal Investment Index, and the correlation of each item with the other five, are shown in Table 2.2. The reliability of the Index is .69, using Cronbach's coefficient alpha.[14] The coefficient represents the average correlation between any split-half subsets of the indicators.

Note in particular the relationship of the Personal Investment Index to its separate indicators. An examination of the relative magnitudes of the part-whole correlations suggests the hypothesis that the items are ordered by the degree of novelty represented by each. The items that best predict the Index are vehicle ownership and nonagricultural employment, which are perhaps the purest

---

*All of the rice mills, stores, and vehicles in these villages were owned by members of the village. The possibility of absentee ownership was checked.

Table 2.1
Sample Variation on the Personal Investment Indicators

	Mean	Standard Deviation	High Score	Low Score
Cultivation of cash crops	62.9% of hh[1]	33.8	100.0% of hh	0
Commercial vehicle ownership	1.6 per 100hh	1.9	8.0 per 100hh	0
Rice mill ownership	1.5 per 100hh	1.0	4.8 per 100hh	0
Store ownership	2.5 per 100hh	1.3	5.3 per 100hh	0
Nonagricultural employment	5.5% of hh	4.5	17.0% of hh	0
Membership in agricultural cooperatives[2]	—	—	—	—

NOTES: 1 "hh" denotes number of households in the village.

        2 The distribution was: 7 villages with no group, 4 villages with an understrength group, and 30 villages with a full-strength group.

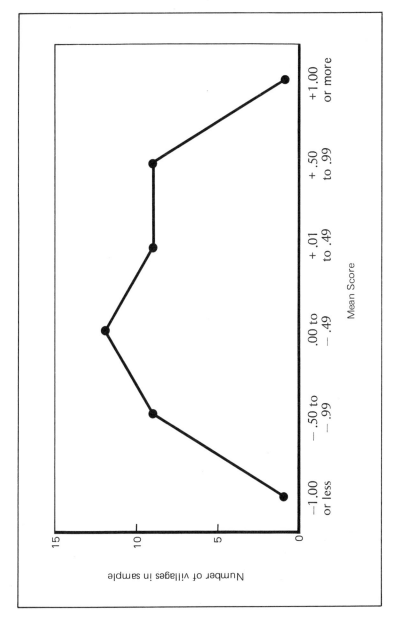

Figure 2.1
Distribution of Mean Personal Investment Index Scores
Among the Sample Villages

Table 2.2

Item-item and Item-index Correlations for the Personal Investment Index

	Membership in credit cooperatives	Cultivation of cashcrops	Store ownership	Rice mill ownership	Commercial vehicle ownership	Nonagricultural employment	CIVIC INVESTMENT INDEX
Membership in credit cooperatives	—						
Cultivation of cashcrops	.20	—					
Store ownership	.16	.25	—				
Rice mill ownership	.20	.33	.45	—			
Commercial vehicle ownership	−.22	.25	.38	.29	—		
Nonagricultural employment	−.03	.17	.15	.52	.56	—	
PERSONAL INVEST-MENT INDEX	.21	.10	.25	.25	.38	.46	—

NOTE: Correlations of items with the index have been corrected for part-whole spuriousness.

expressions of a major degree of investment in new mechanisms for self-improvement. The least related items are cash crop production and credit group membership, both of which are more tentative types of investment, using familiar mechanisms and agricultural practices.*

Taken overall, the statistical characteristics of the Index are appropriate to the rationale that led to the choice of indicators. The substantial reliability (.69) of the Index, given only six indicators, is consistent with the argument that there exists an underlying syndrome labeled "personal investment" that has a number of behavioral outcroppings. The variations in the item correlations with the

---

*Despite the novelty of the label "credit cooperative," use of credit is an old idea in Thai villages. The main novelty of the credit cooperatives has been the notion that it can be desirable to go into debt.

Index follow a pattern consistent with the notion that the substantive content of some indicators is closer to the definition of the investment construct than are others. The Index score will be used almost exclusively, in preference to the separate items, as we go on to explore the relationship of personal investment behavior to modernizing influences and to the governance of the village.

NOTES

1. Daniel Lerner, *The Passing of Traditional Society: Modernizing the Middle East* (New York: Free Press, 1958), p. 438.
2. George M. Foster, "Peasant Society and the Image of Limited Good," *American Anthropologist* 67 (1965): 296.
3. See pp. 61-64 below.
4. Malcolm Quint, "The Idea of Progress in an Iraqi Village," *Middle East Journal* 12 (1958): 372-73. Emphasis added.
5. Frederick W. Frey, "Developmental Aspects of Administration," in *Behavioral Change in Agriculture: Concepts and Strategies for Influencing Transition*, ed. J. Paul Leagans and Charles P. Loomis (Ithaca, N.Y.: Cornell University Press, 1971), p. 269.
6. Lerner, op. cit., p. 48.
7. Samuel P. Huntington, *Political Order in Changing Societies* (New Haven, Conn.: Yale University Press, 1968), p. 32.
8. David E. Apter, *The Politics of Modernization* (Chicago: University of Chicago Press, 1965), p. 10.
9. Everett E. Hagen, "How Economic Growth Begins: A Theory of Social Change," *Journal of Social Issues* 19 (1963): 20-34 passim.
10. Leonard Binder, "The Crises of Political Development," in *Crises and Sequences in Political Development*, ed. Binder et al. (Princeton, N.J.: Princeton University Press, 1971), p. 3.
11. See McClelland et al., *The Achievement Motive* (New York: Appleton-Century-Crofts, 1953); and McClelland, *The Achieving Society* (Princeton, N.J.: D. Van Nostrand, 1961).
12. Foster, op. cit., p. 310.
13. See Appendix A for a discussion of the use of standardized scores.
14. L. J. Cronbach, "Coefficient *Alpha* and the Internal Structure of Tests," *Psychometrika* 16 (1951): 297-334. The equation is

$$a = \frac{k}{k-1} \frac{\sigma_t^2 - \Sigma\sigma_i^2}{\sigma_t^2}$$

where

k is the number of indicators in the index,
σ_i is the standard deviation of the ith indicator, i = 1 to k, and
σ_t is the standard deviation of the index.

CHAPTER

3

PERSONAL INVESTMENT
AND RURAL DEVELOPMENT

Up to this point we have treated personal investment behavior as an accessible and realistic measure of the transition to modernity in villagers. But when the indicators are pegged to expanding aspirations and to manipulation of change, the type of behavior represented in the Personal Investment Index becomes, in some respects, the ultimate objective of rural development programs.

The objectives of rural development programs have not ordinarily been seen in this light. The impact measure of a road-building program has commonly been increases in traffic between village and town; the impact measure of a program promoting hog-raising has been increases in the number of hogs being raised; and so on, with the assessment of the individual program being conducted in isolation from the many others that might be crowding into and around a given village. But, taken overall, rural development programs must in the nature of things be aiming for the kinds of individual initiatives that are captured in the notion of investment of personal resources. There is little choice. Lacking a windfall such as oil reserves, developing countries do not have the national resources to do the job without getting some sort of multiplier effect on their development inputs.[1]

In urban areas, the multiplier may be provided through the private industrial and business sector. In rural areas under totalitarian regimes, the multiplier may be obtained from villagers by a combination of sustained exhortation and the threat of coercion. But for the many countries like Thailand in which the villager is not at all regimented, personal investment behavior is essential as the source of the multiplier. It is therefore of more than academic interest to ask, What causes personal investment?

People start to become modern—invest, in our terms—by being exposed to modernizing influences. That much is unassailable. The problem is to determine

20

what kinds of influences, with what effects. In Thailand since the mid-1950s, the choice is wide. To convey just how wide the changes have been, we have constructed composite portraits of two villages at the extremes. In one sense, they represent the extremes of isolation and exposure to modernity that we observed in the cross-sectional sample. But it is in many ways more accurate to think of them as the modal villages at the ends of the quarter century of change between 1950 and 1975.

THE NATURE OF THE CHANGES

In 1950, the road from village to district town—typically about 20 kilometers away—was probably a cart track, impassable from June to November during the rains and perhaps a full day's trip each way during the rest of the year. The district town itself was only an out-size village, distinguished mainly by its handful of small shops, a police station, and a government office staffed by perhaps half a dozen officials—the chief district officer, a few general-purpose assistants, and an excise and a forestry officer. There were few reasons to visit the district town, even if the journey had been easier.

There was practically no reason at all for anyone to visit the village. The village had few requirements for the goods that a salesman might have to sell, and very little money in any event. A police presence was not provided or desired. Village leaders assumed the functions of constables when peace had to be kept, posses when a stolen buffalo had to be tracked, or judges when a local dispute had to be settled. The official police would have served only to enforce the laws against moonshine whiskey, gambling, and woodcutting, none of which the villagers wanted enforced. Doctoring was available from the local herb practitioner. To the extent that villagers had heard of Western-style medicine, they were skeptical—the rare villager who had gone to a hospital had also usually died. And even electronic strangers were rare: The cheap transistor radio had yet to make its appearance, even assuming that the village was within range of a station. As for visits by a "development worker"—that was an event for which there was not even a name.

The village was extremely "simple." It was a cluster of houses, with a temple and a water source. If you lived there, you were either a farmer or a priest. Only in a very atypical village was there a person who had another full-time occupation. The temple was probably the only source of education. Almost surely no one in the village had been educated beyond elementary school or had obtained any other special training. The only agricultural practices were the immemorial ones.

Life in the village was rough as well as simple. The villagers drank from open wells and very likely suffered widely from yaws, parasites, dysentery, and the occasional cholera epidemic. Malaria was endemic.

In the modal village of 1975, the changes are pervasive. By 1975, the village is almost certainly located on an all-weather road. Probably it carries public transportation several times a day. The district town has several dozen shops, carrying most of the goods sold in a rural American town. There are several drug stores, a few grocers, clothing shops, jewelry shops, and camera shops. There are stores selling agricultural tools, fertilizers, vaccines for livestock, motorized pumps, and the rest of the paraphernalia of modern agriculture.

The government office now has an official for agriculture in general, another one for rice in particular, and perhaps others for livestock, sericulture, or other specialties of the region. It has a health center staffed by a doctor and several nurses. In provinces of the North and Northeast, the government office also includes a Community Development office with one worker assigned full-time to each hamlet in the district.

In the village, there is likely to be a midwife center, or a nearby police outpost, or a canal for tapping a major irrigation system, or even electricity. The village has long since been visited by a doctor, typically one who performed a visible miracle—healing yaws sores in a matter of a few days, with one injection—thereby setting up vast expectations of medical science. In most parts of the country, the village has not seen a case of malaria for several years. Villagers have been exposed in the schools and through health workers to the mechanics of public sanitation and infant nutrition. Possibly the village has a water system and privies. If not that, it has at least one closed well. Probably UNICEF has provided diet supplements for the village's children and the U.S. Agency for International Development (US-AID) has provided prophylactics to help prevent more of them.

By 1975, radios and a variety of stations to choose from have been commonplace for many years. The village has a government-staffed school that teaches at least four grades and perhaps seven. Typically, a few sons and daughters of villagers are attending a secondary school in the district town or the province capital. In a surprising number of instances, the visitor to a village house in 1975 spots a photograph of the king handing a diploma to the villager's son, daughter, brother, granddaughter, nephew, second cousin—someone of the family. It signifies graduation from at least a technical college and probably from a university.

Village leaders have been sent to training courses, sometimes in Bangkok, covering a wide range of topics. Probably at least two of the village's leaders have attended a training course in the administration of the development funds that are being allocated annually to the hamlet.

Added to all this has been contact with a bewildering variety of insurance agents, medicine hawkers, installment-plan sewing machine salesmen, middlemen buying crops, sound trucks advertising a movie or a fair in the district town, researchers, touring government officials, foreigners with the Peace Corps or U.S. military, insurgent recruiters, army units, Border Patrol Police teams,

Mobile Development Units, Mobile Information Teams, Mobile Health Units, and Mobile Vocational Training Units.

Clearly, if a researcher had intruded on the modal village in 1950, the village's score on the Personal Investment Index would have been near zero, while the modal village in 1975 would have scored much higher. Along with the other environmental changes we have described, it is likely that, to at least some extent, villagers in the 1975 village have opened shops, bought expensive milling equipment and very expensive motor vehicles, put land into cash crops, voluntarily gone into debt in order to finance these ventures—all of them, behaviors exhibiting aspirations that could not be inferred from the villager behaviors of 1950. The problem is: Out of the profusion of changes in the village's environment, which ones account for the differences in personal development?

THE CAUSES OF PERSONAL INVESTMENT

Leaving aside the specifics of particular projects, a government in a developing country can affect the nature and quantity of a village's exposure to modernization in two ways.

The first way is to "tutor" the villager through projects that channel him toward new agricultural practices, teach him about modern sanitation and nutritional practices, provide new market mechanisms, or provide him with training in community development or vocational skills. This approach takes as a premise that the villager must the induced to change, and then taught what to change and how.[2] Without that inducement and tutoring, the villager's traditional resistance will persist; or, if he does choose to do new things, he will probably choose the wrong ones. Underlying it all is the notion that the adoption of modern practices is a process that is to be stimulated, overseen, and guided by some outside agent. For convenience, we shall refer to it as *managed exposure* to modernizing influences.

Alternatively, the government can build major elements of the social and economic infrastructure in the countryside and hope for the best. The premise is that contact with the modern world drives the response and that undirected, broad-band influences irresistibly displace the traditional mentality and produce change within a relatively short time.[3] Many of these influences are beyond the government's direct control—the size and sophistication of the nearest district town, for example. But the government can affect the villager's accessibility to the outside world by building roads. The government can also emplace some aspects of modernity in the rural areas by providing schools, health care, police presence, and electricity. In doing so, however, the government that provides the infrastructure does so with very little control over the outcomes. It is contributing to what we shall call *incidental exposure* to modernizing influences: all of those changes that impinge on the villager's perceptions without in any way

being buffered, channeled, or otherwise "managed" to fit his specific circumstances.*

We can recast the question about the causes of personal investment in light
of this framework: Out of the profusion of changes in the village's environment,
managed and incidental, which type accounts for the difference in personal
investment behavior? The quantitative data will be assessed first, followed by
some observations about qualitative factors that help inform the statistics.

Managed exposure to modernization is represented by two variables. The
first is level of community development assistance in baht-equivalent value of
the materials plus cash inputs, over the five-year period preceding the research.
The variable counts any project specifically for the village in question. Thus it
includes potable water projects, credit groups, local irrigation projects, animal
husbandry programs, promotion of any number of specific cash crops, fish pond
construction, day care programs for children, pre- and post-natal nutrition programs, promotion of sanitary privies, provision of vocational training—the whole
range of efforts in health, agriculture, and education that are implemented at the
village level. The variable excludes areawide infrastructure elements such as a
hamlet police station, a government-staffed health center, and other facilities
that may be located in a village but serve a general function for the area (see the
social and economic infrastructure variables below). The second variable
included under "managed exposure" to modernization is the level of training
assistance provided to the village, expressed in mean number of courses attended
by village leaders during the preceding five years. Like development inputs, the
training experiences (515 of them among the sample, ranging from zero to seven
per respondent) covered a variety of fields, from leadership to agriculture to
health. The typical program lasted for three or four days and was conducted at a
district or provincial capital. In many cases, however, the trainees were sent to
Bangkok for courses lasting up to a month. In two cases, a village leader was sent
abroad (one to the Philippines, one to Taiwan) for extended training.

Incidental exposure to modernization is represented by three variables.
The first is accessibility to the outside world, in terms of how long it takes a
villager to reach the district and province capitals, and the size of those towns.
The second is the existence of social infrastructure in the immediate vicinity of
the village, measured by the availability of a health center, school to the seventh
grade (a four-year school is already standard), a police post, a community
center, a movie theater, or electricity. The third variable is the existence of economic infrastructure in the immediate vicinity of the village. Two types of
economic infrastructure are included in the measure: agricultural, in the form of

---

*The use of the word "incidental" is analogous to its use in education, wherein
"incidental learning" refers to all nonschool educational experiences. In both the educational setting and our case, the incidental component can dominate.

a major irrigation system that the village can tap into or a major nearby agricultural project; and nonagricultural, in the form of nearby industrial or agribusiness employment opportunities.

A sixth resource variable is also included: land and water resources, employing a combined measure of soil productivity and natural year-round availability of water. Land and water resources are neutral with regard to modernity—the village has always had them—but they can be expected to facilitate or inhibit the villager's ability to take advantage of the other resources listed above. (Details on the scoring procedures for the variables are given in Appendix A.)

Table 3.1

Intercorrelations of the Exogenous Resource Variables

	Accessibility	Economic infrastructure	Social infrastructure	Government CD inputs	Training programs	Land and water resources
Accessibility	—					
Economic infrastructure	.34	—				
Social infrastructure	.07	.21	—			
Government CD inputs	.06	.14	.40	—		
Training programs	.14	.05	−.08	.24	—	
Land and water resources	.05	.34	.16	−.01	−.34	—

For practical purposes, all six of the variables are causally exogenous to the village's control: The village can do very little or nothing to affect their levels. The occasional exception is found—a village that persuades the government to give it extra development funds, for example. But in general these six variables are most accurately seen as givens from the village's point of view. The intercorrelations among these six exogenous resource variables are shown in Table 3.1.

For purposes of causal analysis, the intercorrelations "should" be zero—that is, the six exogenous resource variables are supposed to be completely independent, uncaused, and unaffected by any other variable in the system under consideration. As an examination of the matrix in Table 3.1 indicates, the six variables are reasonably close to the ideal. Of the 15 coefficients, 11 are nonsignificant. Only four of them are high enough to be significant at the .05 level or higher. Economic infrastructure is significantly correlated with accessibility and with land and water resources, perhaps reflecting the tendency of economic inputs to go to places with good roads and rich natural resources. The other two significant correlations—social infrastructure with community development inputs and land and water resources—reflect a variety of influences. One may be the tendency of community development workers to spend their time in villages that are pleasant places to work (that is, that have the amenities and resources implied by the social infrastructure measure). Another factor is the geographic concentration of training programs in the Northeast, which is also the region with the poorest land and water resources.

To assess the role of the exogenous resource variables in explaining level of personal investment, we start with the bivariate correlations shown below:

	Personal Investment Index
Managed exposure variables	
Government community development inputs	.15
Training of village leaders	.11
Incidental exposure variables	
Accessibility	.38
Economic infrastructure	.44
Social infrastructure	.42
Modern-neutral variable	
Land and water resources	.26

Managed Exposure as an Explanation for Personal Investment

The managed exposure variables are very weakly related to the Personal Investment index. The correlation between the Index and the money spent on community development was .15; the correlation between the Index and the level of government training provided village leaders was .11. For practical purposes, the managed exposure variables have no bivariate relationship with personal investment.

This is another way of saying that the smorgasbord of rural development programs to increase villager income had no discernible relationship with villager behaviors to achieve higher income. This negative finding is subject to two main questions. Do the variables used for the test represent inputs that can reasonably be expected to produce personal investment behaviors? Did the villages in the sample provide a fair test of the relationship?

The answer to the first question must be that the managed exposure variables do capture most of the inputs that constitute the Thai government's attempts to guide village development; moreover, the research was conducted in provinces where those attempts are receiving maximum support in both money and manpower.* The cause-effect relationship between the managed exposure variables and the personal investment should have emerged, if one really did exist for this sample of villages, on two counts.

First, both of the variables include a number of programs that directly and explicitly seek to induce the behaviors measured in the Personal Investment Index—notably cash crop farming and membership in agricultural credit cooperatives. Yet even with these components of the Personal Investment Index, the correlations were near zero. Training inputs were correlated with cash crop farming at .06; with credit cooperative membership at .05. Community development inputs were correlated with cash crop farming at -.15 and with cooperative membership at -.09. These figures are inconsistent with the expectations that led to the inputs.

Even more to the point, the cause-effect relationship between managed exposure to modernization and the Personal Investment Index should hold on indirect grounds. As indicated at the outset of the chapter, rural development programs presumably are intended to elicit population responses that will create multiplier effects on government inputs; and that is exactly what a successful investment accomplishes. The indicators used in the Personal Investment Index signify the kind of self-help efforts that developing rural economies desperately need. In this sense, it is entirely reasonable to expect (again assuming the utility of managed development and inputs for generating economic initiative) that the

---

*Two of the four provinces in the study, Ubol and Nakhon Phanom, have been part of the Accelerated Rural Development program since its inception in 1965. A third, Chiang Rai, was added in 1967, and the fourth, Petchabun, was added in 1968. Because of the insurgent activity in all four provinces, they have also received a wide variety of special economic and social development inputs from other agencies.

summed effects of managed exposure on an overall measure of personal investment behavior should be substantial, because of the carry-over impact from a specific community development program or training session to the villager's general attitude toward change and self-improvement.

For both direct and indirect reasons then, the Personal Investment Index could be expected to correlate with the managed exposure variables if indeed Thai villagers invest because they are prompted to do so by planned programs. The relationship did not exist.

The second question is whether the nature of the sample biased the results. Would the introduction of proper controls expose a concealed relationship between the managed exposure variables and the Personal Investment Index? The rationale for controls is plausible: If the community development and training resources are being concentrated on the most isolated and backward villages (as development policy planners might well choose to do), it is unreasonable to expect dramatic results. In effect, the government's development programs might be bucking the odds by deliberately working in the most difficult villages.

Plausible though the rationale may be, it does not apply to this sample of villages. Drawing from the correlations in Table 3.1, we can see that community development efforts were not being concentrated on inaccessible villages, on villages with especially poor economic infrastructure, or on villages with little social infrastructure.

Similarly, training inputs are not being concentrated on the inaccessible villages (the correlation between level of training and accessibility is .14), or on the economically disadvantaged (the correlation between level of training and level of economic infrastructure is .05), or on those with low social infrastructure levels (the correlation between level of training and level of social infrastructure is -.08). Only one relationship, the tendency of training inputs to go to villages without good land and water resources ($r = -.34$) is consistent with the proposition that contextual variables are concealing the real effects of managed exposure on personal investment behavior. The Thai government's inputs were not being allocated systematically to the poorest and most backward villages of this sample, nor in fact have the principal Thai development agencies ever professed to make allocations on that basis.[4]

It must be emphasized that these comments about development efforts and personal investment behavior refer specifically to attempts to channel and guide village responses, and not to major general-purpose development efforts such as road construction, electrification, or expansion of health and education services. As we shall discuss shortly, these kinds of changes in the environment (which were captured in the social infrastructure variable) are significant in explaining changes in personal investment behavior. It should also be noted that the lack of measurable impact of the managed inputs on personal investment does not mean that they have no impact on the village's capacity to cope with modernization, including some of the problems that personal investment itself generates. These effects will be discussed in subsequent chapters. For the moment, it is simply argued that a common justification for Thai local development programs is that they will encourage Thai villagers to accept change and to use it for their own purposes—to take on a modern outlook, as we have defined it. That justification finds no support in the data for this study.

Incidental Exposure as an Explanation for Personal Investment

The alternative strategy of building a general infrastructure and relying on spontaneous villager reactions is supported by the quantitative data. The correlations of the Personal Investment Index with level of accessibility is .38; its correlation with level of economic infrastructure is .44; its correlation with level of social infrastructure is .42. All of the relationships are statistically significant at the .01 level.

The contrast with the relationship between level of personal investment and the incidental exposure variables is especially striking because of the nature of the independent variables. The incidental exposure variables capture very little that would directly elicit a behavioral response, and yet the statistical relationship is substantial. The extreme example is social infrastructure and its .42 correlation with personal investment behavior. The existence of the facilities included under the variable—health centers, seventh-grade schools, movie theaters, and electricity—are related statistically to apparently "unrelated" behaviors such as proportion of villagers growing cash crops, ownership of stores, and rice mills.

Several explanations come to mind: Social facilities tend to be built in accessible villages, which are also high-personal-investment villages; or social facilities and personal investment both occur in villages with extensive economic infrastructure; or they both occur in villages with good land and water resources. But the correlations of social infrastructure with accessibility, economic infrastructure, and natural resources are .07, .21, and .16 respectively. Controlling for these variables does not appreciably weaken the relationship between social infrastructure and investment. It continues to be plausible to hypothesize that social infrastructure pushes personal investment by changing the villager's way of looking at the world.

Economic infrastructure and accessibility have more direct relationships to personal investment behaviors. They in effect measure the opportunities to invest, and the data indicate that the opportunities were seized often enough to produce a substantial statistical relationship. Conceptually they, like social infrastructure, are mechanisms for connecting the village with the modern world. As such, all three incidental exposure variables should be related to personal investment behavior if we apply the model of rural modernization that sees villager behavioral change as an inevitable consequence of infrastructure development. That they are in fact related is supportive of the proposition that the model fits rural Thailand.

The effects of the three incidental exposure variables were examined in combination through multiple regression. The Personal Investment Index was the dependent variable; the independent variables were accessibility, economic infrastructure, and social infrastructure. The purpose of the exercise was to identify anomalies—the accessible, high-opportunity village that was not showing strong personal investment characteristics, and the isolated, low-opportunity village that was seizing every available change. The overall results (using standardized regression coefficients) were as follows:

$$\begin{array}{l} \text{Personal} \\ \text{Investment} \\ \text{Index} \end{array} = \begin{array}{c} .25\ \text{Accessibility} \\ (t = 1.85) \end{array} + \begin{array}{c} .35\ \text{Social} \\ \text{Infrastructure} \\ (t = 2.61) \end{array} + \begin{array}{c} .28\ \text{Economic} \\ \text{Infrastructure} \\ (t = 1.99) \end{array}$$

$$F = 10.91 \quad R = .604 \quad R^2 = .365$$

These results are not remarkable; they are roughly what would be predicted from an inspection of the bivariate correlations already presented. Using the regression coefficients, "predicted" personal investment scores were calculated for each village in the sample, standardized, and then compared with the standardized observed Index scores.

The most striking result was the scarcity of true anomalies. Even though there was a wide range of actual Index scores for villages predicted to be in the middle of the distribution, there were very few villages which were predicted to be substantially above or below average (in the top and bottom 33 percent of a normal distribution) and failed to meet expectations. Of villages predicted to be in the top 33 percent, all had at least above average Index scores. Of the villages predicted to be in the bottom 33 percent, all but two had at least below average Index scores.

Two villages showed a large enough raw difference between predicted and actual Index scores to warrant examination of the reasons behind their anomalous behavior.

One of the villages had a predicted Index score which would put it in the top 40 percent of a normal distribution. In fact, its Index score ranked fifth from the bottom among the 41 villages in the sample. Its slightly above average predicted score was based on very good accessibility (only five kilometers from a large district town) and a moderate level of social infrastructure (a school to the seventh grade, a police post, and a community center). Its economic infrastructure was poor, mitigated only by the employment opportunities presented by the nearby district town. The reason for the abysmal actual level of personal investment is not obscure: of all 41 villages in the sample, this one was probably the most severely deprived of natural resources. It had no year-round water resources, and exceptionally poor land. The village exemplifies the degree to which extreme levels of poverty can constrain personal investment despite competing influences. In this sample, the relationship is illustrated by one village; for developing countries less generously endowed with natural resources than Thailand, the relationship can be the general rule.

The other village to be considered is a true anomaly. Its Index score was predicted to be in the bottom 18 percent of a normally distributed sample and yet was in fact substantially above average (high enough to be in the top 28 percent of a normal sample). As it happens, the village offers a clear if discouraging example of the conditions under which managed exposure can produce personal investment behavior.

The village was the most isolated village in the sample. Only in the last three years has it been linked to a main highway. It is also isolated from other villages—the nearest one is six kilometers away. In the context of this history of isolation from general contact with modernizing influences, the Thai government decided two years prior to the research to make the village the object of intensive support. It was to be one of three model villages in the district. At about the same time, an army security unit was sent to the village. Somewhat atypically, the sergeant who headed it turned out to be a helpful source of advice about villager problems. Also, the development inputs were needed and well-administered. In two years the village had completed a successful husbandry project, a successful poultry project, a cooperative program for marketing hemp that raised the price reaching the villager, and several other community development projects not directly related to investment behaviors.

In all, the village seems to prove that if a community is isolated from competing incidental modernizing influences, and if the government pumps in unusually large development resources, and if those resources are well administered, and there are other serendipitous circumstances as well, then it becomes possible to identify a direct link between what we have called managed exposure and personal investment behavior. It is not a generally applicable mode.

NOTES

1. The multiplier effects and the general theme of "investment" as a construct for assessing development efforts are discussed in John D. Montgomery, *Technology and Civic Life: Making and Implementing Development Decisions* (Cambridge: MIT Press, 1974), chap. 3. See also Robert E. Krug, Paul A. Schwarz, and Suchitra Bhakdi, "Measuring Village Commitment to Development," in *Values in Development: Appraising Asian Experience*, ed. Harold D. Lasswell, Daniel Lerner, and John D. Montgomery (Cambridge: MIT Press, 1976), pp. 104–32.

2. The most complete single discussion of what we call the tutorial approach to rural development is Conrad M. Arensberg and Arthur H. Niehoff, *Introducing Social Change: A*

Manual for Americans Overseas (Chicago: Aldine, 1964). See also Margaret Mead's introduction in *Cultural Patterns and Technical Change*, ed. Mead (New York: Mentor, 1958). For discussions of peasant resistance to change in the face of a modernizing external environment, see Everett M. Rogers, *Modernization Among Peasants* (New York: Holt, Rinehart and Winston, 1969), esp. pp. 19–49; Joseph Lopreato, "Interpersonal Relations in Peasant Society: The Peasant's View," *Human Organization* 21 (1962): 21–24; John M. Brewster, "Traditional Social Structures as Barriers to Change," in *Agricultural Development and Economic Growth*, ed. Herman M. Southworth and Bruce F. Johnston (Ithaca, N.Y.: Cornell University Press, 1967), pp. 66–68; and E. H. Spicer, ed., *Human Problems in Technological Change* (New York: Russell Sage Foundation, 1952).

3. The classic account of how a traditional value system can shift within a few years is Daniel Lerner's portrait of the Turkish village of Balgat in Lerner, *The Passing of Traditional Society: Modernizing the Middle East* (New York: Free Press, 1958), pp. 19–42. Karl W. Deutsch—in Deutsch, *Nationalism and Social Communication: An Inquiry into the Foundations of Nationality* (Cambridge: MIT Press, 1953) and in his later formulation, Deutsch, "Social Mobilization and Political Development," *American Political Science Review* 55 (1961): 493–514—exemplifies the tendency among many political scientists to assume that modernization in the environment drives personal modernity. Note, for example, that, in his index of social mobilization, indicators of exposure and behavioral response are mixed without distinction.

4. For a description of the allocation process at the district level, see Charles A. Murray, *Thai Local Administration: Villager Interactions with Community and Amphoe Administration* (Bangkok: United States Agency for International Development, 1968), pp. 68–72 and 121–26.

CHAPTER

4

FUNCTIONAL CAPACITY
IN A THAI VILLAGE

The preceding chapters focused on the physical changes that have accompanied the village's encounter with a modernizing outside world, and on the responses of villagers as individuals. Now we turn to an examination of the resources that a village brings to that encounter. Some of these resources are generalizable across villages in Thailand—the overall economic backdrop, general modes of social interaction, and the institutional arrangements. But within this shared framework remain many degrees of freedom. We cluster these other variables under the single label "functional capacity." A strong village—a functional village, in our terms—can provide a variety of supports to the individual villager. It can interpret novel information, provide buffers, develop new rules to fit a changing situation, and enforce old ones that still apply. But functional capacity is a variable quality in villages. To the extent that a village is disabled in performing its functions, it becomes a dead weight or even raises new obstacles in the modernization process. In this chapter, we examine the baseline resources, then the differences among villages as those differences have always existed, long predating modernization. The purpose is twofold: to convey the sense of the difference and to explore an approach to capturing the difference in behavioral terms.

BASELINE RESOURCES

Insofar as the village is the unit of analysis, we concentrate throughout most of the book on points of difference among villages. But there are commonalities, and an understanding of some of the basic ones may be helpful in interpreting the context of the differences. Only the most basic points are covered.

33

The Economic and Social Backdrop

The economic environment has been unusually benevolent in rural Thailand in comparison to other traditional rural societies. The Thai villager has not been forced to use the last foot of tillable land nor to save the last grain of rice. Through happy historical and geographic accident, population pressures have been low. Free land has traditionally been plentiful. Even in the 1970s, tracts of unused land have been available in some parts of the country.* In addition, the soil is usually sufficiently fertile and the rain sufficiently reliable to ensure a steady supply of food. For all practical purposes, famine has been unknown in Thailand, and even periods of widespread food shortages have been remarkable for their rarity. The other basic material needs of clothing and shelter have not been stringent in a country where the temperature seldom drops below 60°F and where wood and bamboo to build the villager's house were until recently effectively free for the taking.

Thailand further deviates from the classic peasant environment in its land tenure system. The tenancy rate has varied among regions and over time, but it has always been low. In 1930 (the year of the earliest systematic economic survey), the number of peasants without land varied from 14 percent in the South to 36 percent in the Central Plain.[1] Overall, a 1949 United Nations Food and Agriculture Organization (FAO) survey estimated that 80 percent of Thai peasants were still working their own land.[2]

The tenancy figures, low as they have been for a peasant society, still do not convey the degree of independence enjoyed by the traditional Thai peasant. Landlords have tended to be absentee, without local agents to surveil the tenants. Resident landlords have been relatively unconcerned about squeezing out the highest rent that the market would bear—often because the landlords were themselves fellow villagers with a few extra *rai*† to rent, and consequently constrained by custom and friendship from pressing their neighbor tenants too hard.[3] Perhaps the most influential factor in maintaining a nonoppressive environment is that a large majority of the villagers in most communities have been independent landowners. The most thorough forms of exploitation such as "company store" or hacienda systems have generally been frustrated by the lack of a local monopoly on land or resources. As a final resort, a villager who found himself in a sufficiently unhappy situation has had the ultimate option of moving to a place where unused land was still available.

---

*Reliable figures are difficult to obtain, because so much of the land that is effectively available is not legally available. It is worth noting that villagers in four of the six districts where this study was conducted had claimed free land within the year prior to the research.

†One *rai* = approximately .4 acres.

The generally benevolent physical environment in Thailand is mirrored in the social and political norms of the village. In most parts of the world, peasants have come to be seen as a stingy, unsociable lot.[4] Thai villagers have been among the few stubborn exceptions. Anthropologists generally continue to conclude that, at least in social terms, Thai villages are pleasant places to live.[5] One way to communicate this fact is to examine the pervasive role of *sanuk*, roughly translated as "fun," in the hierarchy of villager values. As Herbert Phillips points out:

> The importance of sanuk is that it provides the villagers with a standard of value, a measure of how much they wish to commit themselves to a particular activity. . . . Villagers will take on free of charge a major job (for example, helping a neighbor build a house) precisely because it is sanuk. . . . Notice that in this kind of situation there is no overseer demanding the person's effort. His labor is freely given and may be freely withdrawn.[6]

A second way in which Thai villages can be pleasant places to live lies in the personal freedom that is permitted, even encouraged. The highly restrictive limits ascribed to so many village cultures are absent. It is, wrote John Embree, "the first characteristic of Thai culture to strike an observer from the West. . . . The longer one resides in Thailand the more one is struck by the almost determined lack of regularity, discipline, and regimentation in Thai life."[7] The elaborations, exceptions, and objections to Embree's subsequent discussion of Thailand as a loosely structured social system have continued for more than two decades. The core observation, however, that a Thai villager has great social freedom to indulge his preferences, whims, and even eccentricities if he observes just a few basic and elastic social conventions, remains a widely accepted view of rural life there.[8]

Thai villages begin then with economic and social advantages that endow them with potentials and room to maneuver that villages elsewhere seldom enjoy. When we discuss examples of villages with low functional capacity— "disabled" villages—it should not be forgotten that even a Thai village with problems has significant assets.

The Institutional Arrangements

In Thailand, the village is at the bottom of five tiers of civil bureaucracy. Immediately above the village is the hamlet (*tambol*), or collection of villages; next up the ladder is the district, staffed by career civil servants of the central government; above that is the province; and at the top is the Bangkok ministry.

Most villages have three local leaders, who receive a very small honorarium from the government and carry an officially recognized title. These three are the headman, who is elected by vote of the village population, and two assistant headmen selected by him. The several headmen in the villages of a hamlet jointly elect the hamlet chief, called the *kamnan*.

The terms of office for all of these positions have been open-ended. If a village is unhappy with its headman, it cannot be rid of him by waiting for his term to end. It must petition the district officer to hold a new election, then muster a majority of villagers who are willing to vote for removal. In cases of flagrant misconduct, the district officer is empowered to remove the headman by fiat. But unless one of these two courses is taken, the headman continues to hold his job until he dies, voluntarily resigns, or reaches the mandatory retirement age of 60 imposed in 1972.

In addition to these paid, officially recognized positions, villagers may hold one of several other quasi-official posts. In all provinces where the Community Development Department is represented, each village has a village development committee with about seven members. This committee fills much the same function as the earlier "temple committee," a traditional institution that oversaw the administration of civil as well as religious activities in the community.

A village may also have a health committee, agricultural committee, a water association to maintain a communally owned reservoir or dam, a funeral association to provide a kind of "insurance" for funeral costs, or any number of other ad hoc institutions organized by the village or by one of the government's development agencies.

THE NATURE OF FUNCTIONAL CAPACITY

The baseline resources convey little information about the meaning of "good government" or "bad government" in a village. To do that, we will describe two case histories as examples of the extremes. The first represents the acutely disabled village. The second describes a highly functional one. Although the names have been altered, both cases describe actual villages, not composite portraits. In each case, we shall examine the village against three expectations of village government that are commonly cited by villagers as being of chief importance: maintenance of peace and harmony among the inhabitants of the village, organization and leadership of any group efforts that are needed for the public good, and assistance in dealing with the world outside the village.

Case 1: The Disabled Village in a Traditional Setting

The village we shall call Pong is poor and isolated, located in the far northeastern corner of Thailand only a few kilometers from the Mekong River. It has 136 households, an elementary school with two teachers, and a small wooden temple. The leadership structure in the village is simple and traditional, comprised of a headman, his two assistants, and a temple committee. The membership of the temple committee is indeterminate; the village has never formally specified who belongs to it, although there is broad consensus on at least the leading three or four persons.

In governance, Pong represents most of the defects that might plague a traditional Thai village. In each of the three areas that we are using to assess functional capacity, there are serious problems.

Maintenance of Peace and Harmony

Pong has been torn for years by two factions, one headed by a schoolteacher and the other by the headman. A large number of the villagers have joined neither side and wish both of the principals in the feud would go away and leave the village alone. Among other manifestations, the feud has led to accusations that the headman is a communist sympathizer and that the schoolteacher is an embezzler. Rocks have occasionally been thrown against houses of the leading parties in the middle of the night. Worst of all, partisans of one side have been telling the police when a member of the other faction was cutting wood to build a house or making some moonshine whiskey. Both acts are technically illegal (though only sporadically enforced), and the reports led to arrests and fines.

But beyond the disruptions caused directly by the feud, the village is beset by frequent smaller disputes that the headman is unable to resolve. The research turned up several specific instances, usually involving disputes over property boundaries or alleged theft or damage of property. The problem is that, as one informal leader said,

> The headman does not calm down the dispute when he makes his decision. Usually he cannot even decide, so the villagers go to see the kamnan. . . . The kamnan often succeeds in mediating. Sometimes the kamnan sends the persons back to the headman, but they will not go because they have no respect for the headman's decisions.

When villagers talk about going to see the kamnan, it should be remembered that they are referring to a long trip by boat to his village. It is a hard row back upstream, taking the better part of the day. That they are willing to undertake the trip indicates the importance they attach to getting a resolution of the dispute and the low regard they have for the headman's judgment.

Apart from what appears to be a generally low level of competence as a leader, the headman is said to play favorites: "The headman only helps his relatives, and not other people who have problems and go to see him," was one typical response. This is particularly aggravating because "peace and harmony" definitely includes enforcement of laws that villagers want enforced, and one of the headman's relatives is a chicken thief for whom the headman shows too much partiality:

> The headman lectures us at village meetings to look after our children. If anyone behaves like a thief he must be arrested and sent to the police. But when Chan, the headman's brother, was twice caught stealing our chickens, the headman did not do anything when we reported it to him. We had to call the police ourselves.

Leadership of Community Efforts

In this area too, the headman is lacking. Perhaps the clearest example of his incompetence occurred when the villagers were persuaded by the abbot of the temple in the next village to build a brick wall around the Pong temple compound. When a member of the committee broached the subject with the headman, the headman argued against it and raised all manner of problems that might cause the project to fail. He finally gave his consent only after a meeting of the villagers voted in favor of it over his strenuous objections. The wall was completed without his help. "The district officials who visit the village probably think that the work on the wall construction was done well because of the headman's ability," complained one villager. "In reality, the headman did not pay any attention to his work, not even to his official duty."

Liaison with the Outside World

This is especially important for interactions with the district office. Sometimes a villager simply needs advice on who to see to obtain a license or get an identity card. Sometimes he needs supporting documents from the headman. For some types of business, or for a person who is particularly ignorant of the procedures, the headman is expected to accompany the villager to the district office in person. On yet other occasions, the headman would ordinarily conduct all of the business with the district, as a go-between linking the village and the career Royal Thai Government bureaucracy. In all of these functions, the headman of Pong was lazy, incompetent, or both. As one respondent put it when he was asked how he would go about getting help from the district:

> If I want the government to help in anything, I should tell the headman so that he could tell the district official in charge. But this headman is not good. He probably would not go to the district if he were asked. This village is different from other villages, where it is convenient to get things done as needed.

Another respondent, answering the same question, said:

> The headman is the representative of the village. Whatever the villagers need, we should tell the headman, so he can tell the district officials. However, the villagers in Pong believe that the present headman does not try to do anything for us.

The headman is not only inadequate as a representative for making requests upward through the system. The villagers report that he cannot even effectively pass instructions down to the village from the district office. It is said that he always tried to command people, that "he always threatens and shouts at us. Whenever he wants us to do anything, he tries to force us and never asks us nicely."

Not surprisingly, the villagers' low opinion of the headman had repercussions for his ability to conduct the village's business, even when he roused himself to try. From a conversation among village elders:

> Wiang said that he felt ashamed at the meetings of the villagers. He had visited many villages and at meetings the people paid good attention to what the headman said, and were as quiet as if they were listening to a priest. No one argued in the middle of a speech, but waited until the headman had finished. In Pong, whoever wanted to talk did so whenever he wanted. No one listened to the subject of the meeting. . . . Every time that there was an argument the headman would get very angry and shout that the government had appointed him as the leader, and when the leader talked, the villagers had to listen. But the villagers would still argue.

In all three of the basic leadership functions—mediator of disputes, leader of community activities, and intermediary with the district office—the headman of Pong was deficient. But the nonfunctional character of the village spread beyond that. The feud that started between two families had escalated to include nearly everyone in the village, and it paralyzed ordinary actions of mutual help. An informal conversation among men who are considered to be leaders illustrates how far the inability of the village to make self-governing compromises had progressed. One of them, named Sombat, mentioned that a house had been built across the public pathway leading from his house to the main road. This was a plain violation of village protocol. Another villager said that maybe when the soldiers came to visit the village (a regular occurrence), they could be persuaded to tear it down. But Sombat saw another way of taking advantage of the situation. From the interview report:

> Sombat said, "I would like the soldiers to come. When they come, they will tear down any house that is in the way. It would be good

to do that so we will have a pathway to walk on." . . . Then Sombat thought of an idea. His house was across the pathway from Orn's house, a relative who had a big kitchen where they all ate their meals. Sombat said that before the rainy season came he would extend his porch to Orn's kitchen and so not have to go out in the water and mud. He said, "No one could say that I blocked the pathway because the owner of the other house ought to be blamed first."

"Disabled" is a descriptive word for the situation. The villagers of Pong shared the concepts of "good government" held by villagers elsewhere—as in the recognition that there should be a public pathway that one person should not be free to block. But the village lacked mechanisms in good working order for implementing their understanding.

Case II: The Functional Village

The village of Khao Soi is located only 25 kilometers from Pong and is in the same district. It has 104 households, an elementary school, one recently built wooden temple in the village, and an ancient *chedi* (temple tower) about 500 meters across the rice fields. It has no other social facilities.

The leadership structure is again simple: a headman, two assistants, and a seven-man village development committee composed of the same men who were formerly on the temple committee. The governance of the village will be reviewed in terms of the same three functional areas that were used to assess Pong.

Maintenance of Peace and Harmony

Khao Soi had none of the major conflicts that characterized Pong. There were no cliques within the village nor any interfamily feuds. There were quarrels—in the year preceding the research, the headman could remember four inheritance squabbles, two disputes over land and buffalo ownership, three cases of seduction, and several marital spats that were brought to the headman for adjudication. None of these cases was taken beyond the headman, and no evidence emerged that he was ever bypassed in favor of another leader. On the contrary, villagers who discussed the subject unanimously spoke of the headman's good sense in these matters. Law enforcement took care of itself; there had not been a crime during the two years preceding the research.

Leadership of Community Efforts

The major public facilities in the village, the temple and the chedi, were immaculately maintained by a rotation system of volunteer teams. The headman himself led the major ceremonial occasions and gave the largest contributions. The roads within the village were well maintained. The village had constructed a reservoir for irrigation purposes and graded the road into the village from the main highway, both without assistance—monetary or supervisory—from the government. Community funds for maintaining the reservoir were held in a bank under an account held jointly by the headman and two other respected village leaders, using a system of cosignatures to protect the funds from arbitrary use. Part of the cost of renting the equipment to grade the feeder road was paid out of funds raised by selling gravel from a community-owned pit—again, an idea originated within the village. The rest of the cost was paid by contributions, extracted on a progressive basis from the richest families in the village and from those who would use the road to transport goods to the market.

Liaison with the Outside World

In this regard, Khao Soi had a buffer and a "fixer" that had no counterpart whatsoever in Pong. Contrast the following reports from villagers with the earlier accounts from Pong:

When a villager was called to the district office to defend himself against a charge of trespassing, the headman told him what witnesses he would need and how he could find them.

Another villager had rice worms in his field and did not know how to get rid of them. He told the headman, who got a pesticide for him from the district agricultural officer.

Two other villagers gave credit to the headman for getting title to unclaimed land—one because the headman had gone with him to the district land officer, the other because "the headman told me what to expect."

When the district office decided to build a new school for Khao Soi on a site the villagers did not favor, the headman and his assistants prepared a detailed brief objecting to the decision, which the village then submitted in the form of a petition.

The anecdotes are abundant—the inhabitants of Kao Soi enjoy talking about themselves and the way they get things done. All of the stories point to the main conclusion that Khao Soi has exhibited a high degree of competence, imagination, and problem-solving capacity in governing itself. The tasks the village set itself were basic ones, and the apparatus was not elaborate. But the jobs generally got done. The village functioned in ways that Pong did not, and in ways that make a difference in the day-to-day quality of life.

THE BEHAVIORAL TRACE: CIVIC INVESTMENT

The descriptions of the two villages imply a number of behavioral indicators to characterize a given village on the dimension of "functional capacity of the village." Some of them might be "number of trips per month to the district office by the headman," "number of village disputes taken to the police last year," "villager donations to public projects," and so on. But it must be remembered that the data for the two case histories just presented emerged slowly over a month's residence in each village by two skilled Thai interviewers. Only four of the 41 villages of the sample received this treatment. The other 37 were visited by one researcher for only six days each. From them, enough data were collected to give a confident qualitative estimate of the social and administrative environment in the village. But given the peculiarities of village research, attaching numbers to a large set of these behavioral indicators would have been unrealistic, and a large set would have been necessary, because of the differences from village to village in the mechanisms that are used.

Instead, we will focus on the external visible results of being a functional village: evidence of voluntary, continuous, and widespread villager behaviors in support of public goods. The behaviors are labeled "civic investment." The proposition is that the level of civic investment in a village reflects the functional capacity of that village.

The choice of potential unobtrusive indicators is wide. Thai villages not only differ internally, they look different as well. Choosing among the candidates and arriving at appropriate metrics was based on the three key characteristics being sought: voluntarism, continuity over time, and widespread participation among the inhabitants of the village.

The first key element in the logic connecting civic investment and competent self-governance is voluntarism in the behavior. This does not preclude the possibility that social pressure might have been brought to bear—the existence of coherent social pressure is a prerequisite to being a functional village. It does preclude legal obligation or coercion. The distinction is that which exists between donating regularly to a church and paying taxes, and it is an essential distinction for choosing indicators. Thus, to take one common example in Thailand, the amount of village money or labor contributed to a government-sponsored project is not a reliable indicator, because of the uncertainty about whether the villager gave his resources voluntarily or in response to an official request of government officials in charge.

A second key link is the continuity or regularity of the behavior. The one-shot spectacular community project can be misleading. "Functional capacity" is hypothesized to be a quality that elicits steady responses, over substantial periods of time.

The third specification, that the behavior be widespread in proportion to the village population, has a self-evident utility. An impressive action by the village's rich man—in one village, one person paid the entire cost of a new temple—is not indicative of the village's commitment to public goods.

We return then to the question, What do people do in functional villages that reflects the fact of the village's capacity? Four indicators are used as answers, each of which reflects a somewhat different type of functional strength in the community. Details of the scoring for each variable are given in Appendix A.

First, the compounds of the houses in functional villages tend to be cleaner, neater, and generally better-kept than the compounds in nonfunctional villages.* It is an indicator that (with modification for local conditions) probably could be used in communities throughout the world; in effect, it refers to the difference between a community of poor people and a slum. For a Thai village, other manifestations of widespread high morale could be used—for example, the cleanliness of the children's school uniforms might serve. But the condition of the village's compounds is the easiest to observe and rate accurately. Both a high mean and a low standard deviation are positive signs, and the metric (percentage of houses rated above average) gives weight to both characteristics.

Second, the functional village tends to build and maintain internal streets, even if they are only dirt tracks. Access to a street is important to villagers, but it is a facility that one cannot get unless others help. The initial clearing operation and subsequent maintenance require group initiative, organization, and a sense of mutual cooperation. If a cluster of houses is cut off from a street, or if the streets have deteriorated to the point of being impassable, the village is not doing a job that is both surely desired and well within its capacity to perform. The variable is a scale based on the extent of construction and the maintenance of village streets.

Third, a functional village maintains a temple in good condition, whether it is small and made out of bamboo or large and elaborate. A village committee sees to it that the grounds are swept daily, that fences are maintained to prevent animals from entering the temple precincts, and that the walls and roof are sound. If a temple is in disrepair or debris litters the compound, it is safe to assume that it is not because the village has abandoned Buddhism, but because the community cannot muster the organization and cooperation to meet a standard function. The variable is expressed as a score on a trichotomous scale.

Fourth, a functional community will take the initiative in solving local problems through development projects. This is the classic indicator of problem-solving capacity (though in many ways the most unreliable one, unless all the facts about the project are known). For this study, such projects are included

---

*A distinction is important here. The individual house and compound are maintained by the individual householder. Keeping compounds neat is not usually a function of village government, and obviously no conclusions about the governnance of a village can be drawn from the appearance of any one house or even from a small sample. But in the aggregate, villages do unquestionably vary widely in their general appearance, and too widely to ascribe to chance variation. In fact, it was this variance observed impressionistically that first suggested that a village's functional capacity could be inferred through visual observations alone.

only if a reconstruction of the events leading to it indicate that the village, not the government, took the initiative in starting the project. The variable refers to the number of village-initiated projects during the five years preceding the research.

These four indicators comprise the Civic Investment Index.* As in the Personal Investment Index, scores were standardized and then summed to form the Index score. And again, the aggregate Index scores showed broad variation. The distribution of mean scores is shown in Figure 4.1. The plot employs the mean of the standardized scores on the four civic investment indicators.

The intercorrelations among the items in the Civic Investment Index and the correlations between the items and the Index (corrected for part-whole spuriousness) are shown in Table 4.1. The reliability of the Civic Investment Index, again using Cronbach's coefficient alpha, is .56.

Note that the variable for self-initiated development project shows low correlations with the other three indicators. This is in some part an artifact, because village initiation of development projects is inherently restricted prior to exposure to modernization. To this extent, it was guaranteed that isolated villages would have low scores on this component of the Civic Investment Index, regardless of the scores on the other items; hence the correlations with this component were attenuated.

THE VALIDITY OF THE CIVIC INVESTMENT INDEX

The Civic Investment Index is an indirect measure. It does not assess the "thing itself" of good village governance, but rather hypothesized outcroppings of it. The virtues of the approach are the objectivity of the indicators, their unobtrusiveness, and the ease and speed with which they can be collected. Obtaining an Index score for a village with these four indicators is a morning's work for an experienced observer. But the question of its validity must be addressed. Given the indirect nature of the indicators, it is very pertinent to ask of the Civic Investment Index: Does knowing the degree to which a village exhibits the characteristics in the Index provide an accurate estimate of the way that the village goes about governing itself? A comparison of the quantified scores with what was learned about the villager during the residence research suggests that it does.

---

*It should be noted that the items are culture-bound and time-bound. The same indicators cannot be expected to work in other village cultures or in the Thai village culture for all time to come. It is arguable, however, that analogues do exist elsewhere and at all times. The key is a rationale for determining what they are in a specific context.

Figure 4.1
Distribution of Mean Civic Investment Index Scores
Among the Sample Villages

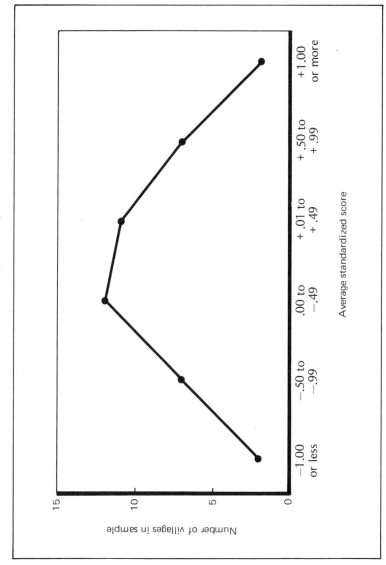

Table 4.1
Item-item and Item-index Correlations for the
Civic Investment Index

	Upkeep of house compounds	Street upkeep	Temple upkeep	Village-initiated development projects	CIVIC INVESTMENT INDEX
Upkeep of house compounds	—				
Street upkeep	.34	—			
Temple upkeep	.25	.44	—		
Village-initiated development projects	.09	.18	.18	—	
CIVIC INVEST- MENT INDEX	.32	.47	.41	.20	—

NOTE: Correlations of items with the index have been corrected for part-whole spuriousness.

First, consider the two villages that were used to illustrate the extremes. Khao Soi, the example of the functional village, had a mean score on the four civic investment behaviors of +.97. It ranked third from the top out of the 41 villages. Pong, the example of the severely disabled village, had a mean score of -.52. It ranked thirty-second from the top. The general consistency of the qualitative indicators of leadership and the quantitative scores in the two villages is clear.

In a parallel fashion, other villages with very high or low quantitative scores also showed obvious and consistent qualitative signs of extremes in functional capacity.

The lowest ranked village of the 41 (with a mean civic investment score of -1.04) is divided sharply into two factions, comprised of those who live south of the road through the village and those who live north of it. The current headman has frequently tried to resign and actually did so for a period of two years, but he was prevailed upon to take office again because none of his successors would keep the job for more than a few months. The headman spends very little time at his job—he is too busy claiming newly opened land 30 kilometers from the village. The only project that the village did complete, a new meeting hall for the temple, provoked open acrimony during the planning meetings, and finally a refusal to participate by people from the north half of the village. Later, it turned out that even the people from the south half of the village could not organize themselves to complete the work. The hall was finished by the youth of the village, working under the orders of the abbot of the temple. As the school headmaster put it, "The people of this village do not like to support each other (*maj chorp snap snun kun*)."

The top-ranked village of the 41 had a score on the Civic Investment Index of 1.51—an extremely high mean for the four standard scores. It also happens to be the only the village in the country with a kamnan who has been awarded an honorary Master's degree in political science from one of Thailand's most prestigious universities.* This is not proof in itself that civic investment be-haviors reflect a high quality of functional capacity—the officials who recom-mended the kamnan for the honorary degree were to some extent influenced by the many development projects and the almost gardenlike appearance of the village that also generated the high civic investment score. But the more data that we accumulated about the village (all four field interviewers and the author were resident in the village, in contrast to the usual lone interviewer), the more it appeared that the village was unusually cohesive and well-governed. Problems seldom even reached the kamnan for resolution; most of them were decided by one of five assistants who had responsibility for different blocks of houses in the village. And in addition to the five block chiefs, the kamnan had developed a system whereby two deputy kamnan were given differentiated responsibilities: one for overseeing the maintenance of the various public facilities in the village, the other for overseeing correspondence with district officials and the status of ongoing development projects. It was a sophisticated system, and it appeared to function well, with a high degree of village support. In no case did we uncover evidence of an undercurrent of opposition to the village leadership, as is often the case for "model" villages discovered by Bangkok officials. This village ap-peared to be as good as its press, and as good as the civic investment score indicated.

More generally, these additional findings bear on the relationship between the quantity captured in the Civic Investment Index and the qualitative nature of village governance.

Of the 17 villages with a negative civic investment score of at least -.25— that is, villages with moderately low to very low levels of civic investment behavior—11 exhibited one or more glaring symptoms of maladroit governance, venal governance, or no governance. In two cases (one of them Pong), there were

---

*The kamnan acted in the role of headman for the village in question. It should also be noted that the village was part of the random sample, not especially chosen because of the kamnan's reputation.

long-standing intravillage feuds that had paralyzed village cooperation. In one, the village leader diverted the money for a bridge that would have linked the isolated other half of the village. Among the 17 villages, there were two cases of removal of the headman for incompetence and another case of attempted removal. In five of them, no donations of money or labor for any development project had been forthcoming during the preceding five years. Headmen in two villages tended to refer minor crimes (such as the theft of a few melons) to the police rather than resolve them in the village. Bribery and fraud were involved in the elections of two of the headmen. In three villages, tensions with a nearby community had developed, to the point of actual fighting in two cases. Reconstruction of development events showed that projects in four of the villages had deliberately been designed to give preferential treatment to an influential subgroup within the village. And to a greater or lesser extent in several of the villages, villagers who were logical choices for leadership positions were avoiding them when possible.[9]

The 11 villages in the middle range of scores, from -.24 to +.24, showed mixed indications. The Civic Investment Index appears to have relatively little discriminating power for this type of village: Some villages with a minor negative index score seemed from a qualitative assessment to have greater functional capacity than other villages with a minor positive score.

For the 13 villages with moderate to high civic investment scores (greater than +.24), the Index again appeared to have predictive utility. The clearest sign is that there was not a single instance of a noticeable grievance. In none had the village petitioned for the removal of the headman; in none had there been discernible village feuds; in none did we find evidence of corruption on the part of any village leader; in none did we find evidence that a subgroup within the village was getting preferential treatment. Going beyond these negative indications is difficult: Impressively high functional capacity has fewer strikingly obvious symptoms than disability in a village. High capacity instead tends to manifest itself through a series of small successes and village characteristics that require a more extended description. Villagers talk enthusiastically of their headman, or make invidious comparisons of other villages with their own. On numerous small matters, they cite the headman or village elders as the last word. Development projects get done. News is disseminated. And, to an observer, the village leaders come across as being thoughtful about village problems and energetic in attacking them. The villages where these collections of small indications were consistent also did well on the indicators of civic investment.

Our best summary of the qualitative validation is that the Civic Investment Index appeared to have substantial value for this sample as a measure of functional capacity. The predictive power of the Index is greater for villages outside the middle range. Once outside that range (roughly, the middle 20 percent of a normal distribution), the Index for this sample was accurate in identifying high and low levels of functional capacity.

NOTES

1. Carl C. Zimmerman, *Siam: Rural Economic Survey, 1930–31* (Bangkok: Bangkok Times Press, 1931), p. 26.

2. National FAO Committee on Thailand, *Thailand and Her Agricultural Problems* (Bangkok: Thai Ministry of Agriculture, 1949), p. 18. For historical background on Thai agricultural landholdings, see G. A. Marzouk, *Economic Development and Policies: Case Study of Thailand* (Rotterdam: Rotterdam University Press, 1972), pp. 128 ff.; and James C. Ingram, *Economic Change in Thailand Since 1850* (Stanford, Calif.: Stanford University Press, 1955), chaps. 2 and 3.

3. Kamol Janlekha, cited by Herbert P. Phillips, *Thai Peasant Personality: The Patterning of Interpersonal Behavior in the Village of Bang Chan* (Berkeley and Los Angeles: University of California Press, 1965), p. 19. Janlekha further argues that, given the rentals and crop values in the Central Plain, a villager may be better off renting than owning.

4. This has been a theme ever since Oscar Lewis, in *Life in a Mexican Village: Tepoztlan Restudied* (Urbana: University of Illinois Press, 1951), fragmented the earlier consensus that peasants lived a familial, almost Rousseauean existence. A few examples from many in the subsequent literature are S. C. Dube, *Indian Village* (Ithaca, N.Y.: Cornell University Press, 1955), Clifford Geertz, "The Rotating Credit Association: A 'Middle Rung' in Development," *Economic Development and Cultural Change* 10 (1962): 241–43; Gerardo and Alicia Reichel-Dolmatoff, *The People of Aritama* (Chicago: University of Chicago Press, 1961); and, probably most famous of all, Edward C. Banfield, *The Moral Basis of a Backward Society* (Glencoe, Ill.: Free Press, 1958).

5. Phillips, op. cit., is one of the best. For studies focusing on North Thailand, Reginald le May's *An Asian Arcady: The Land and People of Northern Siam* (London: Cambridge University Press, 1926) is still worth reading, as are Michael Moerman, *Agricultural Change and Peasant Choice in a Thai Village* (Berkeley and Los Angeles: University of California Press, 1968) and Moerman, "A Thai Village Headman as a Synaptic Leader," *Journal of Asian Studies*, May 1969, pp. 535–49. Other useful descriptions are Lauriston Sharp et al., *Siamese Rice Village: A Preliminary Study of Bang Chang 1948-1949* (Bangkok: Cornell Research Center, 1953); Howard K. Kaufman, *Bangkhuad: A Community Study in Thailand* (New York: J. J. Augustin, 1960); and nearly all of the articles in Hans-Dieter Evers, ed., *Loosely Structured Social Systems: Thailand in Comparative Perspective* (New Haven, Conn.: Yale University Press, SEA Studies, Cultural Report Series no. 17, 1969).

6. Phillips, op. cit., pp. 59–60.

7. John F. Embree, "Thailand: A Loosely Structured Social System," reprinted in Evers, op. cit., p. 4.

8. See Evers, op. cit., for an overview of the consensus, and James N. Mosel, "Communications Patterns and Political Socialization in Transitional Thailand," in Lucian W. Pye, ed., *Communications and Political Development* (Princeton, N.J.: Princeton University Press, 1963), pp. 184–228.

9. See pp. 68–80 for a discussion of the factors surrounding these symptoms.

CHAPTER
5

EFFECTS OF MODERNIZATION
ON FUNCTIONAL CAPACITY

The behaviors we have called personal investment and civic investment are at once similar and unlike.

They are similar in that they all represent initiative and goal-directed behavior on the part of villagers. Growing a cash crop, buying a rice mill, learning nonagricultural skills, or joining with neighbors to build a road, beautify the village, solve a community problem—all are evidence of a villager's willingness to take affirmative action in pursuit of some value.

The two types of behavior are unlike in the nature of the values and in the instrumentalities by which the values are realized. Personal investments tend to be highly individualized. The return not only accrues to the individual; it is usually the individual acting alone who gets the job done. Civic investments not only yield returns that are available to the community as a whole, but also typically require group action, cooperativeness, and interdependence.

The similarity argues for the hypothesis that the two types of behavior should occur together, permitting a village to be placed on a single dimension of "goal-directed activity," including items from what are now called the Personal and Civic Investment Indexes. It is intuitively appealing to hypothesize that villagers who show intelligence and initiative in governing their community will show those same qualities in dealing with opportunities for personal improvement. The difference between the two types of investment argues for the hypothesis that the two will not occur together. Private and public goods have not been mutually reinforcing in most cultures. More often, private interests have been competitive with public goods in ways that have prompted restraints on entrepreneurial activity.

In this chapter we examine the issue in light of the data from the 41 villages of this study. As personal modernization occurs in the form of personal investment behavior, what happens to the functional capacity of the village?

The bivariate relationship between the Personal Investment and Civic Investment Indexes conveys very limited information. The correlation was almost zero (.02), and the inter-index item correlations were uniformly low as well. They are shown in Table 5.1.

The results clearly support the utility of examining goal-directed behavior in terms of separate indexes for the public and private dimensions. The items in the two indexes do not tap a common underlying syndrome when observed at a single point in the village's development history. But neither is it apparent that the two types of behavior are competitive. The villages in the sample were sometimes rated high on both personal and civic investment, as well as low on both or high on one and low on the other—just as the .02 correlation implies.

The key point is that the observations for both indexes are taken at a single point in the village's development history. The correlations denote relationships that exist when a cross-sectional slice is taken from a dynamic process. More specifically, the relationships are complicated by the fact that functional capacity existed before modernization began, and so did a high degree of variance in functional capacity among villages. Premodern Thai villages were not on a uniformly high plane of self-governance that is now being degraded by modernization—as illustrated by Pong, a miserably governed village that had

Table 5.1
Inter-index Correlations for Indicators in the Personal and Civic Investment Indexes

	Temple upkeep	Street upkeep	Upkeep of house compounds	Village-initiated development projects	CIVIC INVESTMENT INDEX
Cultivation of cash crops	−.04	−.26	−.06	.17	−.02
Membership in credit cooperatives	−.01	−.18	.15	.03	.00
Store ownership	−.07	−.19	.22	.17	.06
Rice mill ownership	−.13	−.32	.25	−.04	−.08
Commercial vehicle ownership	−.07	−.03	−.05	.17	.01
Nonagricultural employment	.19	.03	−.04	.02	.07
PERSONAL INVESTMENT INDEX	−.03	−.26	.16	.15	.02

hardly been touched by modernizing influences. But existence of variance in the premodern case also means that the current variance in civic investment for isolated villages cannot be explained by the influence of modernization or investment. Or, in other words, by including villages in the sample that have low levels of modernization, we have guaranteed a great deal of noise in the system when we try to identify a relationship between modernization and functional capacity. So the correlation between the Personal and Civic Investment indexes may mean exactly what it says most directly—modernization and functional capacity have no systematic relationship. Or it may mean that the true effects of modernization take time to show themselves, and the survey cut into the process at an early stage.

Our reading of the data suggests that the latter proposition is more accurate. In the following discussion we present evidence that incidental exposure to modernization and the resulting increases in personal investment lead to three sets of consequences.

One set of consequences involves the increasing heterogeneity of income and interests within the village, which increases the stresses on the village political system.

Another set of consequences involves the increasing imbalance between the rewards of private investment and public positions, which tends to discourage time and attention to leadership duties and which diminishes support from the population for community efforts.

The third set of consequences deals with the concentration of leadership positions among an economic elite within the village, whose members naturally gravitate toward one side of the newly emerging interest conflicts.

These three sets of consequences reinforce each other. The net effect is that unchanneled exposure to modernization, and particularly investment, tend to reduce the functional capacity of villages. The natural course of events—that is, in the absence of countervailing public policy—is argued to be an accelerating deterioration in functional capacity as modernization spreads.

We shall be drawing on a variety of evidence, some quantitative and some qualitative, some hard and some that is frankly speculative. The qualitative aspects of the presentation will be framed by the use of a causal map. The word "map" is used to distinguish it from a causal model, which has a specific technical meaning. The map is a way of summarizing the argument: It contains brief, nontechnical and nonquantitative statements of the principal events in the causal chain, presented diagrammatically. It will be presented in pieces at the conclusion of the presentation of each major component of the argument. Its primary purpose is heuristic, to show how the components of the process fit together.

Accompanying the causal map will be a path model.* It is in effect an

---

*For details see Appendix A and its notes.

operational overlay for the map. Following exactly the same causal directions and linkages, it inserts the quantitative counterparts of the variables in the map wherever quantification was judged to be feasible. But the path model is not complete in itself; it should always be examined against the backdrop of the more complete causal map. The model only summarizes the relevance of the quantitative relationships to the full exposition.

The reason for this procedure is that the argument from the entire body of data is substantially richer than the argument from the quantitative data alone. The steps in the process that we have been able to measure with numbers bridge intervening qualitative variables in some cases, and stop short of the most interesting outcomes in others. To some extent, those statements are still true of most of the important topics in the social sciences. But they are particularly relevant to this topic, because we are describing a process that takes place over an extended period of time, and one that has barely gotten started in some of the villages of the sample. The early steps in the process—the ones toward the left-hand side of the causal map—have occurred in almost all the villages; the ones in the middle of the process have occurred in some of the villages; the ones at the end of the process have occurred in only a handful of villages with a long history of exposure to modernization.

It is argued that the latest steps have occurred only in those villages because of the length of exposure to modernization required to produce them—it makes sense that they were scattered in occurrence, according to the theoretical outlook. But in practical terms it means that the "sample" of villages in which we can expect to observe the ultimate outcomes is far less than 41. An attempt to quantify would have produced variables on which 38 or 39 villages would score zero, every time. So the best quantitative measures are available for variables that are first-order outcomes in point of time and (usually) in significance. The more ultimate outcomes, and the most important ones, are also the ones that occur latest in the time sequence and hence tend to be the ones for which we have the least systematic data.

With these comments about the presentation in mind, we are ready to start tracing the links between personal modernization and the functional capacity of the village.

THE CAUSES OF PERSONAL INVESTMENT (RECAPITULATION)

The discussion of personal investment and its causes argued that a relatively simple causal sequence effectively explained the aggregate personal investment behavior in the villages of the sample: Villagers were exposed to modernizing influences through the development of economic and social infrastructure in the local environment, and increased accessibility increased the

Figure 5.1

Causal Map of the Links Between Incidental Exposure to Modernization and Personal Investment

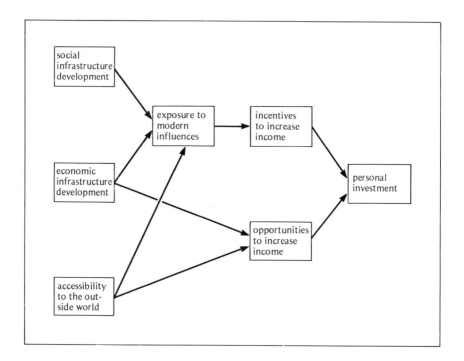

opportunities to improve one's lot in life; all three types of exposure increased the incentives to do so. The result was the type of risk-taking self-improvement behavior we have called personal investment. Diagrammatically, the causal sequence may be displayed as shown in Figure 5.1. The path model corresponding to that diagram is shown in Figure 5.2.

Figures 5.1 and 5.2 bring us to the first of the three major causal sequences flowing from unchanneled exposure and investment: increased heterogeneity of economics and interests within the village.

Figure 5.2

Path Model of the Operationalized Variables Linking
Incidental Exposure to Modernization with Personal Investment

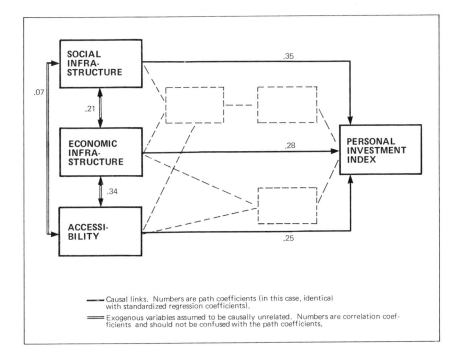

LINE I: INCREASED HETEROGENEITY WITHIN THE VILLAGE

The initial stress on self-governance has its origins in the intrinsically risky nature of personal investment. Nowhere is personal investment universally successful. In a village with a high personal investment score, a great many of its members are actively trying to make money. Some succeed and get richer. Others fail and do not get richer; perhaps they lose money, and become poorer. Inexorably, personal investment increases economic disparity within the village if the previously better-off invest as actively as the previously poor.

Over and above the increases in disparity caused by investment are the factors in incidental exposure to modernization that tend to raise villager income unevenly. A new road happens to pass one villager's land, an an oil company buys a piece of it for a filling station. A new irrigation system reaches one villager's land, and not his neighbor's. A new pineapple cannery is built near the village, and hires 15 village girls out of the 100 who may have wanted the jobs. These new opportunities brought by modernization are invariably distributed with a large helping of luck. And along with the opportunities to improve one's situation come the opportunities to be tricked, conned, and otherwise manipulated by outsiders. Accessibility to the outside world is a double-edged resource.

These facts of life about personal investment and modernization in all but the most thoroughly controlled developing economies are reflected in high correlations with the measure of economic disparity used for this study, based on variation in the quality of housing within a village. More formally, the variable is expressed as standard deviation of a village on the combined ratings for size of house and expense of materials of the house: In Thai villages, people with more money tend to put some of that money into their houses, making them larger and fancier.* People without money live in very small, cheap huts. The variable thus serves as an unobtrusive proxy measure of disparities in economic status within a village.

The correlations of economic disparity with the antecedent variables in the model are as follow:

	Intravillage Economic Disparity
Accessibility	.42
Economic infrastructure	.53
Social infrastructure	.38
Land and water resources	.42
Personal Investment Index	.57

The correlations are high with all of the antecedent variables, and highest of all with the Personal Investment Index, reflecting (we argue) the kinds of uneven gains that have been described. The correlations with economic infra-

---

*Unlike villagers in some other traditional societies, Thai villagers do not try to conceal wealth. There is no social opprobrium attached to being better off than one's neighbors.

structure and accessibility are hypothesized to be direct causal links. The correlation between disparity and social infrastructure is hypothesized to reflect an indirect causal link: The development of social infrastructure has no effects on income directly, but the existence of the infrastructure causes the investment behaviors that in turn contribute to economic disparity.

Note that the variable for natural land and water resources of the village also significantly related to economic disparity (r = .42). Presumably this relationship has held true since periods antedating modernization. Good soil and plentiful water have attracted competition for land, and subsequent disparities in distribution of wealth, in traditional and modern societies alike.

The causal relationships we have been discussing are summarized in Figure 5.3, which begins where the previous causal map left off. The corresponding path model follows in Figure 5.4.

The importance of increasing economic disparity depends in part on the way in which it is taking place. A situation of simultaneous enrichment and impoverishment among the extreme income groups has different implications than one in which disparity is increasing because some are getting richer faster than others but everybody is getting richer.

The shape of the increasing disparity is treated as an entirely empirical issue in this study. The approach to modernization that we have presented lays down no constraints on whether everybody "should" in theory get richer, or the rich get richer and the poor get poorer. In order to explore the question, two additional variables were scored, using the same observations of house size and expense that were the basis for the disparity variable.

First, a variable was developed to estimate the size of the bare-subsistence population in each village. It denotes the percentage of houses rated "3" or less on both size and expense, using the nine-point scales for each data point. Translated into more concrete terms, a house that scored low enough to qualify as a unit of this variable was made out of leaves or mats, and was on the order of ten feet square, or less in size. It is substandard housing, even by Thai village standards.

A second variable was developed to estimate the size of the clearly surplus-product population in a village. It denotes the percentage of houses rated "7" or higher on the scales for both size and expense. A village's houses included in this rating were solidly made of wood or masonry and typically had a large porch and three or four rooms.

The correlations of substandard housing and superior housing with the antecedent variables in the modernization sequence are shown below.

Figure 5.3

Causal Map of the Links Between Modernization and Increases in Economic Disparity Within the Village

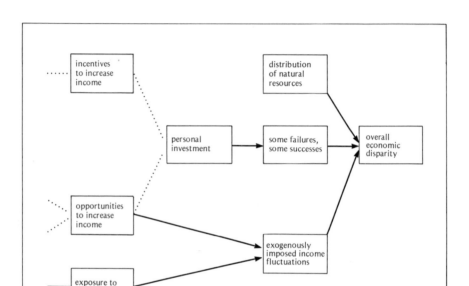

	Level of Superior Housing	Level of Sub-standard Housing
Land and water resources	+.20	−.25
Social infrastructure	+.25	−.04
Economic infrastructure	+.53	−.24
Accessibility	+.34	+.15
Personal Investment Index	+.62	−.37
Intravillage economic disparity	+.77	−.19
Level of superior housing	—	−.46

Figure 5.4

Path Model of the Operationalized Variables Linking Modernization and Economic Disparity Within the Village

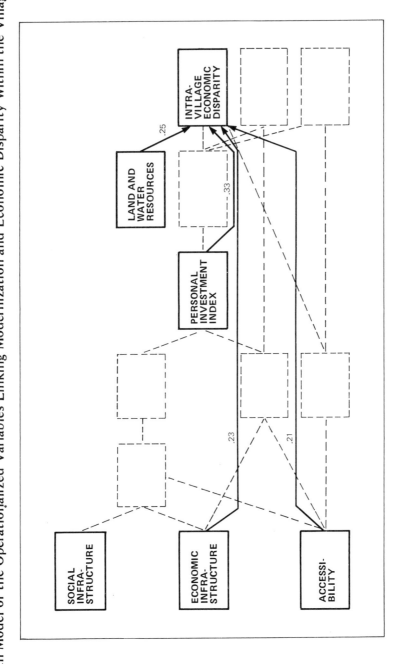

The correlations suggest that the increase in economic disparity is being generated by increases in the number of families at the upper end of the income scale rather than by increases in the number of very poor families—compare the very high .77 correlation between economic disparity and superior housing with the negative (-.19) correlation between economic disparity and substandard housing. Interpreted optimistically, personal investment could be argued to reduce the number of families in the lowest strata; disparity is increasing only because the progress of those families is not as rapid as the progress of the higher income levels.

The bivariate relationships are better seen in the context of the relationships in the next segment of the causal map (Figure 5.5). We have been

Figure 5.5

Causal Map of the Links Between Modernization and Changes in the Relative Sizes of the Extreme Income Groups Within the Village

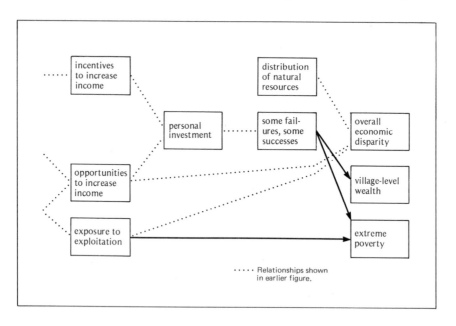

suggesting that the trigger for increasing disparity is exposure to incidental modernizing influences and the personal investment behaviors that follow from those influences. Disparity does exist in the premodernizing village when natural resources are high, but it is argued that the dramatic changes—the villager who gets rich or loses everything—are more characteristic of the village that has entered into the modernization process.

The logic of the sequence just described is summarized in Figure 5.5. Note that no causal arrows link overall economic disparity with "village-level wealth" and "extreme poverty." They are more accurately conceived as representing different foci of the same general phenomenon—distribution of wealth within the village—than as discrete conditions that "cause" each other. As before, the causal map is followed by its operational analogue in the forms of the path model (Figure 5.6). Coefficients shown in earlier diagrams are omitted to aid readibility of the figure.

Interpreted causally, the path coefficients shown in Figure 5.6 suggest that the personal investment process in rural Thailand is serving to increase the number of surplus-income families and reduce the number of marginal subsistence families at approximately the same rate overall (p of the Personal Investment Index with superior housing is $+.47$; p of Personal Investment Index with substandard housing is $-.49$), but not at the same rate within each village—remember the Personal Investment Index's .57 correlation with economic disparity. In any given community, the villager's perspective on the phenomenon is likely to lead him to conclude that some villagers are being left behind economically.

Note also that the development of economic infrastructure has a positive relationship to superior housing ($p = +.30$) independently of the path through personal investment, indicative of the latent utility of infrastructure. Building a dam that provides year-round irrigation to an area (to use a common type of input that was counted in the economic infrastructure variable) should increase the productivity of even traditional farming behaviors, apart from the investment uses made of the new irrigation resource.

A final implication of the path coefficients, and one that should be of interest to development planners, is that the double-edged nature of increased accessibility was statistically evident for this sample of villages: Accessibility to the outside world in this model had only a trivial effect on the number of surplus-income families ($p = +.06$) but also a substantial relationship to the number of marginal subsistence families (p of accessibility with substandard housing is $+.34$). In fact, accessibility was the only antecedent variable in the path model that showed a positive relationship to substandard housing.

We turn now to social heterogeneity. The premise linking the discussion with economic disparity is that social relationships among neighbors change as economic relationships change. When a community is economically homogeneous, an important source of competitiveness, class distinction, envy, and conflict

Figure 5.6

Path Model of the Operationalized Variables Linking Modernization and the Relative Sizes of the Extreme Income Groups

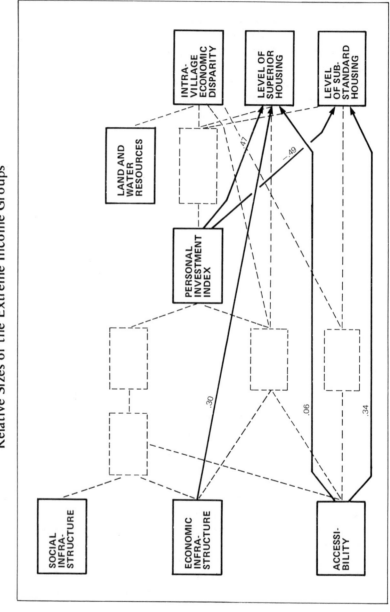

of interest is absent. As economic heterogeneity increases, so does the incidence of those undesirable social phenomena. The premise is far from new to this study.

Because we did not gather systematic attitudinal data, we do not know the extent or the exact nature of changes in social perceptions as economic differentiation within the village increases. Conversations with villagers on related topics suggest (not surprisingly) that villagers themselves do not consciously perceive changes in social interactions occurring because of economic changes within the village. There were, however, two observational indications that such changes might already be taking place.

In villages with low personal investment scores, income groups appeared to be scattered randomly about the village. This held true even if the village had high levels of economic disparity. A large, solid house might be found next to the smallest mat shanty in the village. This economic formlessness in the layout of the village generally characterized villages up through the average and somewhat above-average personal investment levels. But in villages with very high levels of personal investment behavior as scored on the Index, housing patterns often did appear, with distinguishable high-rent districts and a wrong side of the tracks. In one community divided by a main highway, all of the small, mat houses were concentrated on one side of the road; all of the large wooden houses were on the other side. In another village, the poorest houses were concentrated on a hill. In a third, all of the best houses lined the road; the further back from the road, the poorer the house.

Inquiries revealed that the phenomenon was not the result of recent in-migration by poor outsiders. The poor families had roots in the village as deep as the richer ones. Either they had "always" been poor or they had recently suffered some misfortune, miscalculation, or both, which had resulted in the loss of the family's landholdings. A typical case was one young couple living in a small leaf hut on the outskirts of the village that had the second highest personal investment score out of the 41 villages. The husband's father had sold his land for what had seemed a fortune, with the intention of purchasing cheaper land elsewhere. But the cheaper land durned out to be more expensive than he thought, and some injudicious purchases ate into the capital, and now the son and his wife work as hired labor for other farmers in the village.

A second indication of changes in social relationships within the village is found in evidence of demoralization among the bottom economic stratum. Using the data from the house-by-house observational survey of each village, we asked how many of the economically substandard houses also showed extreme signs of neglect in upkeep. The quality being sought in an observational variable was the slum syndrome: the state of not only being poor but also feeling poor as well, without optimism that anything can be done to change the situation. The variable is technically defined as the percentage of substandard houses that were also rated three or lower on the nine-point scale of compound upkeep. Qualitatively, this means a small mat shanty and compound littered with refuse and showing other signs of neglect—rips in the mats, broken steps on the porch, uncleaned utensils—which could have been corrected even without money. The houses included in this unobtrusive measure of demoralization were in sharp contrast to others in the survey that were as small and flimsy but meticulously maintained.*

The bivariate correlations of the demoralization variable with the antecedent variables in the path model are as follows:

	Evidence of Low-Income-Group Demoralization
Land and water resources	+.11
Social infrastructure	+.12
Economic infrastructure	+.00
Accessibility	+.19
Personal Investment Index	+.24
Intravillage economic disparity	+.18
Level of superior village housing	+.22
Level of substandard village housing	+.10

The bivariate correlations are low. But as in the case of substandard and superior housing, we are primarily interested in the patterns of relationship when demoralization is hypothesized to be a consequence of increased socioeconomic differentiation within the community. A detail of the causal map (Figure 5.7) shows the argument. The corresponding path model is shown in Figure 5.8.

Interpreted causally, the path coefficients suggest provocative conclusions. Simple economic disparity did not in itself push demoralization among the lowest-income groups, as long as the disparity was concentrated within the middle-income ranges. Instead, the path coefficients suggest, it was imbalances at the extremes and particularly at the rich extreme that were the primary sources of the apparent don't-give-a-damn behaviors among the very poor: The path coefficient running from "superior housing" to "low-income-group demoralization" was a substantial +.41, while the coefficient running from economic disparity to demoralization was not even positive.

----

*This slum syndrome variable will later be analyzed conjointly with the Civic Investment Index. Because one component of that Index is the measure of overall village upkeep of compounds, the question arises whether the demoralization variable and the Civic Investment Index are confounded. They are not, given their use in this analysis. A detailed discussion of the issue is included in Appendix A.

Figure 5.7

Causal Map of the Links Between Income Distribution
and Social Stresses Within the Village

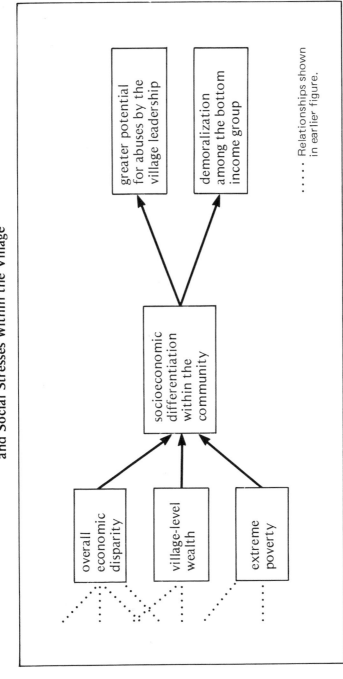

Figure 5.8

Path Model of the Operationalized Variables Linking Income Distribution and Social Stresses Within the Village

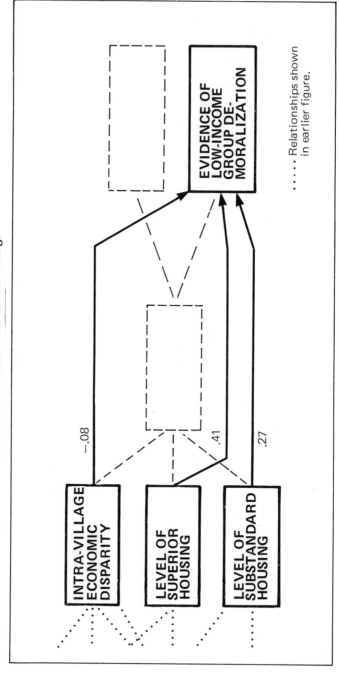

This completes the first of three lines of argument connecting incidental exposure to modernization with outcomes that are stressful to the village as a political and social community. We have focused on villagewide effects: changes in the structure of the village. Now we turn to the second line: the effects of modernization on leaders within the village—who might ordinarily be expected to counteract the disruptive tendencies we have been describing.

LINE II: THE INCREASED VALUE OF TIME

We return again to the far lefthand side of the map, to the point at which the villager has been exposed to modernizing influences. This time the analysis concentrates on the individual villager who does decide to invest for himself. The key consequence, we argue, is that the value of time increases for the personally investing villager. Even after the subsistence harvest could have been sown, reaped, and stored, he has work to do. As the headman cited earlier said, he can no longer just sit around during the dry season—there are too many things to buy in the stores.

Nor does time become more valuable only during the dry season. When the villager has decided to supplement his subsistence rice crop with a cash crop, a part-time job, or one of the other sources of extra income, his hours lengthen during the growing season as well.

A number of unquantified, anecdotal indications were encountered that villagers are busier than they used to be. One was unavoidable, emerging as a by-product of trying to conduct village research: the availability of villagers for interviews varied with the village's level of personal investment. In a low-investment village during the dry season (when all of the field work was conducted), it was easy to find a number of male adults relaxing or doing minor chores around the house compound. In high-investment villages, these potential respondents were much scarcer. Particularly if the respondents were village leaders, it turned out that they were in the fields working with a dry-season crop or were in the district town on business. Another indication was the emptiness of high-investment villages during the house-by-house survey. It occurred to us too late to include, but another useful variable for the observational survey would have been "percentage of houses with a male adult at home." Much more companionship was available during the tour in communities with low levels of personal investment.

The reduction of leisure time is in itself a major change for a people who often call sitting quietly, doing nothing, *nang len*—"sitting for fun." To speed up the pace of Thai village life is to change one of its most fundamental characteristics. But the increased value of time has as well a number of consequences directly related to governance of the community.

When time takes on value, it becomes harder to justify contributing labor to build a neighbor's house, or to dig a roadbed, or to help track down a buffalo thief. There is less time to help design a new temple or to prepare the decorations for a community ceremony. If one man's time has more value than another's, a simple trade of time for purposes of mutual help becomes "unfair" and so it becomes more reasonable to hire or to sell labor than to exchange it or to contribute it.

The switch from donated labor to cash equivalents was apparent in the case histories of development projects. In Thai village development, it has been customary for some years to set the labor component of a project in terms of contributions per household: so many cubic meters of dirt to be dug per household, or so many clay bricks fired per household, or so many days of labor per household. If a villager does not want to do the work himself he is free to hire someone else to do it for him. But only occasionally did villagers in a traditional setting actually do so—money was too scarce. In high-investment villages, the option generally appeared to be increasingly popular. At the extreme, it had become an unvarying practice: The three villages rated highest on the Personal Investment Index had not undertaken even one project in the last five years that involved a general contribution of labor by the members of the community.

In theory, the substitution of money for labor does not necessarily cripple the village's capacity to undertake community projects, but it does in practice, by raising the cost of contributing. The traditional commodity—time during the dry season—had been extremely low cost. It had also been perishable. The time spent repairing a road for the village could not have otherwise been stored and used during planting when time was precious. The new commodity, money, is manifestly valuable and nonperishable. The cash used to hire someone else to repair the road could otherwise have been stored and used to buy help during planting. Because the cost is higher, villager support for community projects tends to become more fragile and more susceptible to interruption.

A clear example of this occurred in a village with a very high level of personal investment that decided four years ago to build a simple wooden temple. The project had been sustained entirely by money contributions; no villager had donated labor. At the time of the research (after four years, for a simple project), the job was almost done. All that remained was to nail up the boards for the side of the temple. The lumber was already at the site, the nails were at the site—and the work was at a standstill because, the headman said, the temple committee could not collect enough money to hire someone to nail the boards in place. Why not just collect a few volunteers and finish off the work? Because, he replied, no one would agree—the villagers had no time. Voluntary labor support from the population at large appeared to have become a thing of the past for that community.

A second and even more important consequence of the increased value of time lies in its tendency to siphon off the talents of the potential leadership group of the village.

The position of headman is expensive and time-consuming. So also to a lesser degree are the other leadership positions in the village. A leader is not only expected to be on call for any villager, any time; he also must expend serious money (for a villager) in the course of pursuing his official duties—entertaining visiting officials, paying for his own uniform, donating example-setting amounts to village projects and festivals. The honorarium that the headman and his two assistants receive seldom covers expenses. The only compensation has been the respect and prestige that go with the jobs.

In the traditional village, such compensation was usually enough to ensure that the most able men in the village occupied recognized positions as leaders— not always, by any means, but usually. And, in every village, including the most traditional ones, the same complaints have been heard that being a leader is a burden, a constant source of aggravation, a duty from which the respondent would like to be relieved. These protests are sometimes genuine, sometimes a polite way of demonstrating a proper level of reluctance to seek power. But regardless of the complaints, to be a good headman or a valued adviser has traditionally meant that the incumbent was obligated to serve. Resignations have been rare.

In villages with leaders who are active in personal investment, the already high traditional costs of being a village leader go even higher. At the same time, the sources of obligation and satisfaction apparently become less compelling. In a number of cases, successful and enthusiastic village investors were finding village leadership to be an unacceptably expensive luxury. They tended to use one of three remedies: refuse to serve at all, serve without devoting much energy to it, or serve and use the position for private profit.

The evidence for the first option, refusing to accept positions, usually emerged by accident. While staying in the village, an observer would notice that one obviously well-off villager played no leadership role, ask why, and find that the man in question had refused all nominations to official positions and dis-couraged an informal role as well.

Another indirect indication that able men were refusing positions surfaced in responses of villagers to the question, "Why was X chosen for his position?" In villages with low and moderate scores on personal investment, the answers tended to be, "He is a smart man," or "He is a pious man," or "He is a good talker." In one way or another, the repondents addressed the question of qualifications for the job. In villages with high personal investment scores, an answer was frequently given that was not heard in the other villages: "He was chosen because he has spare time."   ·

Finally, there was the occasional very direct statement of the relationship between personal investment and unwillingness to serve. The clearest of these examples was the headman who resigned his position after three years in office, then resumed it two years later. He was asked to explain the gap. He replied that he had quit in order to make money. He had a son whom he wished to send to secondary school in Bangkok, and being headman took too much of his time. Later, when the son was already in school, the villagers prevailed upon him to become headman again. He had agreed, reluctantly, but was once again trying to resign. The stated, explicit reason was to have more time to invest in his livelihood.

The evidence for the second option, serving without devoting much time or energy to it, was comprised of two types. First, it was noticed that assistant headmen in villages with high levels of personal investment tended to have substantially fewer duties than men in the same positions in a lower-personal-investment village of the same size. Assistants in the high-personal-investment villages tended to give nonspecific answers to questions about their function— "I help the headman in whatever he needs"—which upon further examination turned out to be another way of saying that he did nothing much at all. In the top-ranked village on the Personal Investment Index, a harder indicator was available: The two assistants had a rotation system, one month on and one month off. There was not, said the headman, enough work to keep both of them busy. In contrast, assistants to the village headman in the lower-ranked villages on personal investment more often listed specific, regular duties. Sometimes these were fit within a relatively complex administrative framework: one assistant for administration of daily affairs, another for overseeing the organization of villagewide projects; or, in one case of a village on the bank of the Mekong River, an assistant to keep track of the night guard-duty roster for the boat pen. Sometimes the village had independently instituted these kinds of divisions of labor, sometimes they had been instigated by a community development worker. The main point is that "lack of work" for leaders seemed to be concentrated in the high-investment villages.

A second type of evidence that village leaders in high-investment villages were reducing their work load emerged from the narratives that were obtained about settlement of disputes and petty crime. Of all the headman's duties, that of keeping peace from day to day ranks high, and perhaps highest, on most villagers' list of priorities. As was noted in the discussion of the functional village (Chapter 4), it was consistently cited as a primary source of satisfaction or dissatisfaction with a headman's performance. Moreover, it is one of the most critical functions from the government's perspective—if the provincial courts system is to function at all, it is essential that the village weed out all but the most important civil disputes and criminal offenses. It was thus of special significance that headmen in villages with high personal investment appeared to be readier than their more traditional counterparts to send villagers to the hamlet police station or district office when petty crimes and disputes arose. Again, it must be emphasized that we are dealing with cases in the villages with the highest personal investment scores in the sample, when the headman or another respondent in these villages would occasionally tell of a case being referred to the police or the district, which, in less modernized villages, would have been

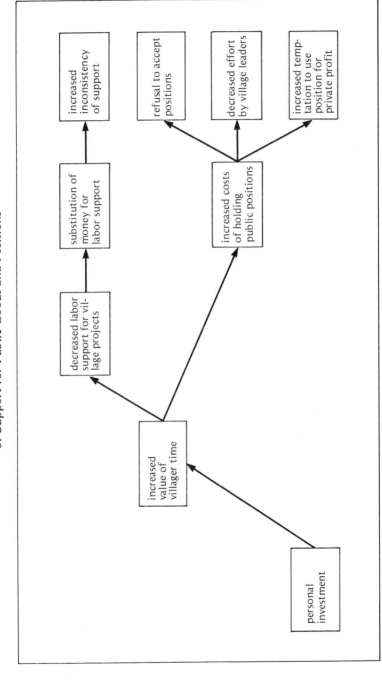

Figure 5.9
Causal Map of the Links Between Village Investment and Deterioration
of Support for Public Goods and Positions

personal investment

increased value of villager time

decreased labor support for village projects

substitution of money for labor support

increased inconsistency of support

increased costs of holding public positions

refusal to accept positions

decreased effort by village leaders

increased temptation to use position for private profit

71

settled locally except in the most extraordinary circumstances. The incidence was not high. The curiosity is that the police were ever called in, when the issue was one that would result in a reprimand if settled in the village but a jail term if taken to the police. It suggests an indifference not only to the village's traditional leadership functions but to the leader's constituents.

Up to this point we have argued that a sequence of events following from investment occurs roughly as shown in Figure 5.9.

The third option resulting from the increased costs of holding public office, "increased temptation to use position for private profit," will be discussed subsequently, with the material on economic elitism within the village.

There is no corresponding path model for the diagram in Figure 5.9. The nature of the evidence was anecdotal and descriptive, as the preceding discussion indicated. None of the elements was susceptible to quantitative treatment through the available data.

LINE III: CONCENTRATION OF LEADERSHIP AMONG AN ECONOMIC ELITE

The first line of the causal chain ended with the argument that personal investment and exposure to modernizing influences work in tandem to produce socioeconomic differentiation, which in turn increases the potential for conflicts of interest. This potential is heightened by the leadership's entanglement in the differentiation. The third line connecting incidental exposure to modernization with deterioration in the village's functional capacity continues to focus on the leadership group—now, with the emphasis on their economic position in relation to that of the average villager.

Thai villagers traditionally have respected wealth and chosen their leaders partially on the basis of economic standing within the community. In view of the money costs associated with some of those positions, it has not been an unreasonable criterion. But the more persuasive consideration appears to be that a man smart enough to be headman or a committeeman also should be smart enough to maintain a prosperous household.

As already noted, modernization and investment are apparently being accompanied by substantially increased economic disparity; moreover, the disparity is being generated in the villages of the sample primarily by the enlargement of the upper-income groups. The result is that the villager who always tended to pick his leaders partially on the basis of wealth now has a larger and more clearly delineated "rich" group of villagers from which to choose. Even if those men are also becoming more reluctant to accept village offices, the net effect is that leaders tend to be chosen from among an economic elite of successful investors.

Two separate assertions are involved, and each was susceptible to quantitative tests. The first is that leaders are being drawn from among the successful investors. Two measures of personal investment behavior among leaders were devised. First, it was asked what proportion of the leadership group had moved away from agricultural subsistence farming. The variable that resulted is a calculation of the percentage of village leaders whose predominant source of income is nonagricultural. The second variable is concerned with innovative agricultural investment as well as commercial investments. It is an estimate of income from "new" nonsubsistence, noncrop sources—for example, from livestock, poultry, sericulture, rental of agricultural equipment, or other agribusiness ventures as well as from owning a store or a bus.

The correlations between nonagricultural employment, personal investment income among village leaders, and the antecedent variables in the causal chain are shown below:

	Percentage of Leaders in Non-agricultural Employment	Noncrop Leadership Income
Land and water sources	.06	.18
Social infrastructure	.18	.21
Economic infrastructure	.29	.27
Accessibility	.35	.15
Personal Investment Index	.42	.52
Intravillage economic disparity	.39	.57
Percentage of leaders in nonagricultural employment	—	.66

The bivariate correlations support the view that personally investing villages tend to choose personally investing leaders ($r = 0.42$ for the Personal Investment Index with nonagricultural employment among leaders) and, more importantly, they tend to choose successful investing leaders ($r = 0.52$ between the Personal Investment Index and leaders' investment income; $r = 0.66$ between nonagricultural employment among leaders and leaders' investment income).

The second assertion is that the gap between leaders and led is increasing as well. This proved difficult to test directly in the absence of detailed information on mean wealth among the nonleader population in a given village of the sample. The data did permit an indirect test.

The only available economic datum about the general village population was the mean landholding of a random sample of 10 percent of the households in each village. In order to use landholdings as the basis for a comparison of leader versus nonleader wealth, two complications had to be dealt with. First, increments of one unit of land mean different things in different places. The leaders in village X may have three times as much land as the average villager in

X, but be very little richer if the land is unusable scrub. The leaders in Y may have only 25 percent more land than the average villager in Y, and be much richer—if their extra holdings are rich lowland bordering a river.

Second, most successful personal investors were designated as leaders by the respondents in the village, despite frequent reluctance of those men (as noted earlier) to accept the headman or assistant positions in very high personal investment villages. But these same men, who are often the richest men in the village, also frequently have very small amounts of land—their money is being made from the market, not the rice fields. The comparison of leaders and non-leaders on landholdings misses that source of wealth, and most of it is concentrated among the leader group. The result is severe underestimation of real leader wealth, particularly in villages with high proportions of leaders engaged in nonagricultural employment.

The first problem was not amenable to a wholly satisfactory solution. It was, however, substantially reduced by the following procedure. The mean and standard deviation of landholdings among the random sample of heads of household were calculated for each village. Then the mean landholding of the leader group for that village was expressed as if it were a standardized score based on the parameters from the random sample. The resulting "proxy z-score" was used to estimate the magnitude of the economic gap between leaders and nonleaders, measured in terms of landholdings.*

The landholding-based variable attempts to estimate the magnitude of the average difference between leader and led. A second variable is needed to measure the extent to which leaders are being drawn exclusively from an above-average income group. The second variable we developed was percentage of leaders whose landholdings are larger than the mean landholding of the random sample. Again the landholding data have to be used, and the same cautions apply.

The place of the two variables, *magnitude* and *extent* of economic elitism, in the chain of events leading to deterioration of functional capacity is squarely in the middle of the other two lines. At the same time that socioeconomic differentiation is occurring within the village, and at the same time that the

---

*Mathematically, the variable is an evaluation of the following expression:

$$\frac{\text{mean leader landholding} - \text{mean villager landholding}}{\text{standard deviation of villager landholdings}} \quad \text{by village.}$$

It is called a "proxy" z-score because the leader landholdings were not included in the data used for calculating the standard deviation (because leader landholdings are likely to be unrepresentative, and thus bias the estimate of the villagewide mean and standard deviation).

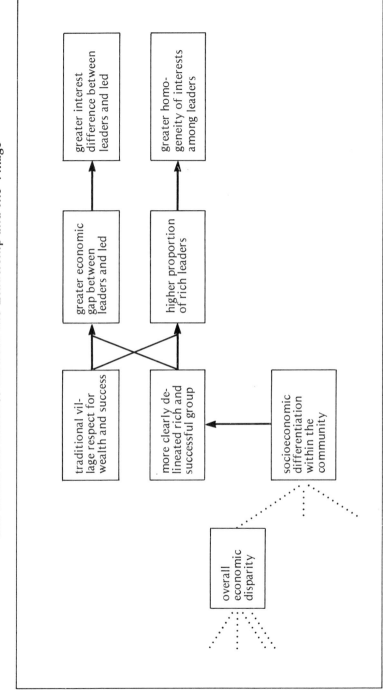

Figure 5.10

Path Model of the Operationalized Variables Linking Economic Disparity and Economic Distance Between the Leadership and the Village

leaders' commitments of time and energy and enthusiasm are diminishing, two economic trends within the leadership group make it less likely that they will respond to the new problems or resist new temptations. First, their economic interests become more widely separated from those of the village as a whole; second, their own intragroup interests become more homogeneous. The hypothesized sequence of events is shown in Figure 5.10.

The correlations of the extent of leadership domination by an economic elite, and the magnitude of the gap between them and the rest of the village, with the rest of the variables in the path model are shown below. With only a few exceptions, the correlations are insignificant, consistent with the earlier discussion about the limitations of landholdings as a measure of wealth. Some of the very rich leaders have very little land. Many of the sources of noncrop income require very little land. In this kind of situation, the path coefficients become particularly useful. The operationalized aspects of the diagram in Figure 5.10 are shown in the continuation of the path model (Figure 5.11).

	Percentage of Leaders in a Landholding Elite	Magnitude of Landholding Gap Between Leaders and Village
Land and water resources	+.20	+.30
Social infrastructure	+.24	+.08
Economic infrastructure	-.10	-.20
Accessibility	+.11	+.02
Personal Investment Index	+.05	+.12
Intravillage economic disparity	+.15	+.13
Level of superior housing	-.09	-.04
Level of substandard housing	+.40	+.24
Noncrop leadership income	+.27	+.08
Percentage of leaders in nonagricultural jobs	-.02	-.18
Percentage of leaders in a landholding elite	—	+.60

As expected because of the statistical artifact, percentage of nonfarmer leaders has a negative relationship to the measure of economic elitism among leaders. But the measure of mean leader income from noncrop sources does show a strongly positive relationship with economic elitism. For the reasons discussed above, it can be assumed to be a conservative estimate. Even without that assumption, the path coefficient is supportive of the argument that the leaders of modernizing villages are decreasingly representative economically of the village as a whole.

Figure 5.11

Path Model of the Operationalized Variables Linking Economic Disparity and Economic Distance Between the Leadership and the Village

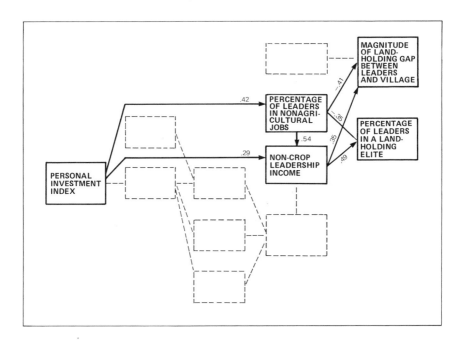

A SYNTHESIS

The outcomes stemming from incidental exposure to modernization, and particularly personal investment, begin to interlock. The same forces that lead to a greater potential for intravillage conflicts of interest also tend to produce a leadership that has a vested interest on one side of those conflicts. The same

Figure 5.12
Consolidation of the Outcomes Leading Directly to Deterioration in Functional Capacity of the Village

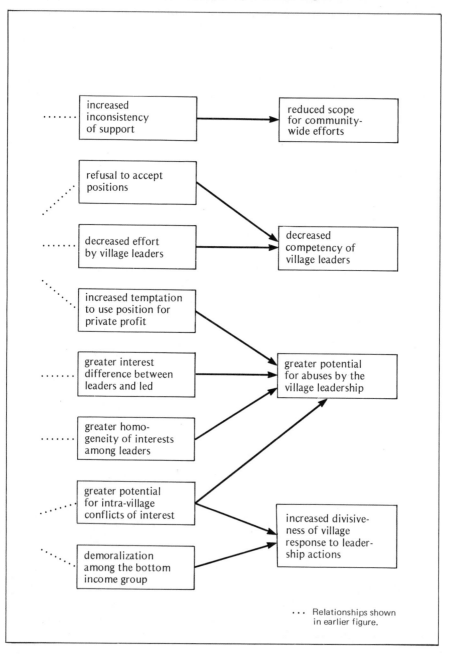

phenomena that make it more expensive for villagers to devote time to community efforts also make it less likely that their leaders will ask sacrifices from
them. At the same time that the lowest-income groups in the village are likely to
be demoralized by the increasing gap between them and their more fortunate
neighbors, the leaders who could serve to counter that demoralization are
exposed to greater temptations than ever before to use their positions for their
own benefit, not the community's.

Eight separate negative outcomes shown in previous diagrams are listed
together and consolidated into four categories in Figure 5.12. These are the
ultimate outcomes from the modernization sequence, and the ones that are
argued to occur relatively late in time as well. Evidence touching on some of
them—inconsistency of support, refusal to accept positions, decreased effort by
village leaders, demoralization—has already been discussed. But we have yet said
little about perhaps the most disrupting of all the outcomes—"greater potential
for abuses by the village leadership"—for that outcome is not a product of any
one line of the chain, but draws from all three of them.

The problem should not be confused with the occasionally corrupt headman
who can appear in any context, modern or traditional. Rather, the question is
whether the dynamics of modernization are tending to subvert the integrity of
village leadership. Presumably the best place to test the hypothesis would be in
villages near Bangkok, exposed to modernization much longer than the villages
in our sample. But even in the 41 villages, a few signs are worth citing.

Consider as an example the village with the highest personal investment
score among the 41 in the sample. During the last five years before the research,
it had completed only one project on its own: a concrete dam thrown across a
stream near the village. Only one project in five years is in itself well below the
average for the sample (the village's civic investment score was sixth from the
bottom), but the more important inferences come from the nature of the project
and the way it was carried out.

The dam diverts most of the flow from a stream that runs through the
fields of many villagers but does not (in its natural course) provide water for the
wealthier members of the community. They were the sponsors of the dam
project, and they carried it out themselves, without participation by other
members of the village. They also maintain it through the mechanism of a
"water association," a type of group responsibility for maintenance of irrigation
systems that is common throughout many parts of rural Thailand. The dam has
the effect of sharply reducing the supply of water available to villagers who do
not have access to the irrigation system. The same men who built the dam also
happen to hold the leadership positions in the community: All of the men designated as leaders are members of the water association. They also live in a single,
clearly defined part of town, along the main highway.

The dual facts of their leadership positions and proximity as neighbors
may have had a bearing on a second project that was being considered at the

time of the research. The Electric Authority had advised the headman that the village could tap into the main electrical lines running along the highway, and gave him an estimate of the cost required to string wires through the village. The village committee met to consider the Electric Authority's estimate. And it was decided that stringing wire to all of the houses in the village would be too expensive and too much trouble. Why not just wire the houses along the road, where it was easy and cheap? So the members of the committee get electricity; the rest of the village does not.

In another village with high personal investment, the houses of the community are divided by a river. There is no bridge. It also happens that all but one of the official positions are filled by people who live on the side of the river that has access to a road. Three years ago, budget money for a bridge was offered by the district office, and a health center was built in its place.

The decision to build the health center instead of the bridge may or may not have been in the best interests of the village as a whole. It is certain, however, that it was in the headman's best interests. He is himself an active investor, and ambitious for his children. One of them, a daughter, had been sent to school for training as a midwife. She will now come back to work in the health center that was built instead of the bridge, and make several hundred baht a month—or so her father expects—even though the official salary for a midwife is only a fraction of that. The advantages of this situation for the headman are freely pointed out by the people who live on the other side of the river.

Examples like these are not black and white. Decisions are being made on the basis of normal human self-interests. None of the three projects above involved a sin as simple as graft. Instead, it is suggested that they are glimpses of the kinds of problems that follow from the chain of events we have been outlining in these pages: for a variety of reasons, modernization and personal investment increase the opportunities and the inclination to use village positions to further personal interests.

The correlations of the expression of village functional capacity, the Civic Investment Index, with the rest of the variables in the model are shown below. The three correlations significant at the .01 level are civic investment with size of the bare-subsistence population (-.45), with concentration of leadership positions among an economic elite (-.32), and with existence of a slum outlook among the poorest segments of the village (-.61). Two of those three variables are directly linked to civic investment in the path model, which operationalizes—to a very limited and proximate extent at this point—the causal map. The third variable with a direct link to civic investment is the measure of the magnitude of the economic gap between leaders and the village at large. The path coefficients are shown in Figure 5.13.

	Civic Investment Index
Land and water resources	−.11
Social infrastructure	.00
Economic infrastructure	−.01
Accessibility	−.16
Personal Investment Index	+.02
Intravillage economic disparity	−.04
Level of superior village housing	+.10
Level of substandard village housing	−.45
Evidence of low-income group demoralization	−.61
Percentage of leaders in nonagricultural jobs	+.17
Noncrop leadership income	+.03
Magnitude of landholding gap between leaders and village	−.23
Percentage of leaders in an economic elite	−.32

Figure 5.13

Path Model of the Operationalized Variables
Leading Directly to Civic Investment Behavior

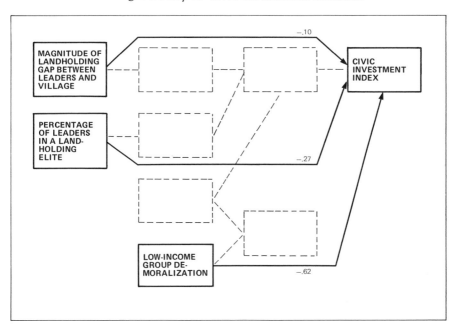

Of the three variables, demoralization among the poorest strata of the villages has the most strongly negative relationship with the village's functional capacity. How much this coefficient would drop if the feedback loop were calculated is unknown; certainly it would drop to some extent, since low levels of functional capacity must reinforce the demoralization process.

The measures of economic differences between leaders and led were only moderately associated with low levels of civic investment behavior and together account for only 10.1 percent of the variance in the Civic Investment Index.

The -.45 correlation between civic investment and size of the bare-subsistence population is not matched by a direct causal link in the map, and consequently it is not in the path model either. The map focused on the relationship of modernization in particular to village functional capacity. Poverty in itself is not new to the modernizing era, and presumably it has always been detrimental to functional capacity. Disregarding its irrelevance to the special concerns of the causal map, the bivariate correlation makes very good sense. It also may help answer the question, What were the causes of variance in functional capacity prior to the onset of modernization?

In a purely statistical sense, the three variables argued to be encouraged by modernization and directly debilitating to village functional capacity explain 48.0 percent of the variance in the Civic Investment Index. When a fourth variable, the size of the bare-subsistence population, is added into the equation as a generally negative influence on functional capacity in both the traditional and modern cases, 55.8 percent of the variance in the Civic Investment Index is explained.

But as we stressed at the outset of the analysis, the latest stages in the interaction between incidental exposure to modernization and functional capacity are also the ones for which the quantitative data are most tenuously representative of the dynamics hypothesized to be at work. To conclude that we can "explain" 48 percent or 56 percent of the variance in functional capacity is both to overstate and to understate the situation. It is an overstatement in that the correlations do not represent wholly one-way causation and in that the operational variables do not fully represent the constructs in the causal map. But it is equally an understatement: Eight outcomes were argued to be encouraged by the modernization process, and to be directly inimical to a village's functional capacity. Only three of those eight were even incompletely expressed in quantitative form.

The presentations of the causal map and the path model are finally completed in Figures in 5.14 and 5.15, as all the pieces from the separate diagrams are shown together. They represent a summary of all the many ways in which modernization has been argued to work against functional capacity. That leaves open the question to be addressed in the next chapter: What makes functional capacity increase?

Figure 5.14

The Completed Causal Map Linking Modernization With Reduced Functional Capactity of the Village

Figure 5.15

The Completed Path Model Linking Modernization With
Civic Investment Behavior

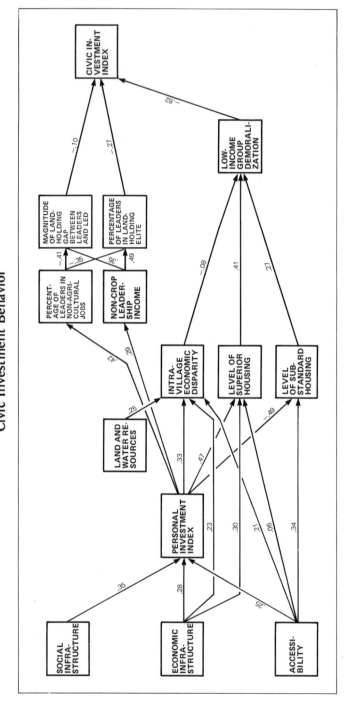

CHAPTER

6

EFFECTS OF DEVELOPMENT
POLICY ON FUNCTIONAL CAPACITY

We have just described what might be called "the natural course of events" for rural modernization. Developing countries like Thailand naturally tend to build infrastructure in the form of schools and health centers, roads, and electrification and irrigation systems. Economic opportunities from the private sector naturally tend to expand into the rural areas, and the growth of district and provincial towns naturally tends to bring urbanlike influences to formerly isolated areas.

These were the inputs that went into the calculation of the quantitative variables used in the analysis. None of them was significantly, positively related to the measure of functional capacity, civic investment. Or, to put it another way, the data indicate that there is nothing in the natural course of modernization that works in favor of good village government. The highest positive correlation between the Civic Investment Index and the 13 antecedent variables in the model was .17.

On these ground alone, it is immediately provocative that what has been called "managed exposure" to modernization is significantly, positively related to the Civic Investment Index. The Index's correlation with community development inputs was +.35, and its correlation with training programs for village leaders was +.37. Moreover, the relationship between managed exposure and functional capacity was most conspicuous for villages at the higher levels of incidental exposure to modernization, as shown in Table 6.1.

When we interpret the numbers in the table, development and training inputs for this sample had these effects: If the village was relatively isolated from incidental exposure, managed inputs were associated with a modest rise in functional capacity, from a -.07 mean civic investment score to a +.14 mean score. But the change was so modest that it was almost no change at all; remember the comments in Chapter 4 about the insensitivity of the Civic Investment Index to

Table 6.1
Mean Civic Investment Scores for Contrasting Types of
Exposure to Modernization

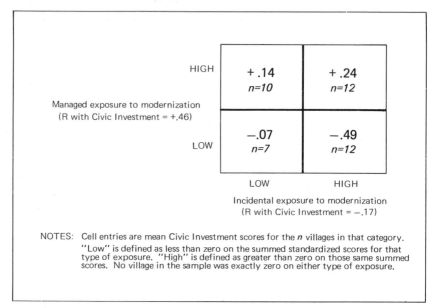

NOTES: Cell entries are mean Civic Investment scores for the *n* villages in that category.
"Low" is defined as less than zero on the summed standardized scores for that
type of exposure. "High" is defined as greater than zero on those same summed
scores. No village in the sample was exactly zero on either type of exposure.

qualitative differences in functional capacity when small increments are involved. But for villages rated "high" on managed exposure to modernization, it
made a clearly noticeable difference whether the village had or had nor received
managed inputs—from a -.49 mean civic investment score for villages low on
managed exposure to a +.24 mean score for villages that were rated high. The
implication, and a surprising one in view of managed exposure's nil effect on
personal investment behaviors, is that the natural course of events in
modernization does bring on a sharp drop in functional capacity, but one that
the intervention of government inputs can not only brake but reverse.

To state the implication assumes that the relationship between managed
exposure and the civic investment is a causal one. This must remain speculative
in any event. But if we make the assumption, it should be possible to identify
the mechanisms at work that make sense of the causal link. What is it about
development and training inputs that raises the civic investment measure of a
village's functional capacity?

The logical first answer is that the inputs are doing what the Thai government thinks they are doing: teaching villagers new techniques through the training courses, and giving them practical experience through the administration of
development projects under the tutelage of the government's community
development workers. It is a new variation of the notion that development can

be guided and managed, an idea examined earlier in relationship to the adoption of personal-investment practices.

A second explanation will be considered as well: that the provision of development inputs and training programs interacts with the characteristics of village leadership—not in an educational sense, but by altering the content of being a village leader, and by evoking responses that would otherwise cease to occur as modernization in the private sector proceeded. To put it simply, we will suggest that development assistance raises the stakes for village positions, and keeps them vital and competitive with the distractions of personal investment.

TUTORED DEVELOPMENT REVISITED

Some aspects of managed exposure do in fact have an intrinsic tutoring, guiding component. Many of the training programs deal with subject matter that is unfamiliar to villagers. Many of the development projects use technology or concepts that are unfamiliar to villagers. So insofar as the training instructions are remembered and the technology is understood, the tutorial explanation should have some validity. But it cannot be taken for granted that either of these effects occurs with regularity.

Training Programs

It is extremely difficult for a person who has observed village training programs and their aftermaths to persuade himself that the educational component accounts for the statistically significant correlation between them and the Civic Investment Index. As a first objection, only half of the programs that went into the calculation of the training variable had anything to do with village self-governance. Of the 515 training experiences reported by the leader respondents, only 240 (46.6 percent) were general leadership training (most of them for the Developing Democracy Program or for village development committee training). Another 20 (3.9 percent) dealt specifically with health or education but could be presumed to have relevance to leader decisions in those areas. The other 49.5 percent were concerned with agricultural innovations, technical training, and a wide variety of topics related to economic improvement—all of which would tend to promote the personal, not civic, investment score.

Beyond this consideration, the training experiences that did deal with leadership skills were not necessarily learning experiences, Often, respondents told us that they had not even understood the presentations, because the speakers had used central dialect. The central dialect is understood by most Northern and Northeastern village leaders when spoken slowly and applied to everyday subjects. But the respondents typically told us that, when it was spoken rapidly and about unfamiliar topics, they could catch only the gist of the speech, if that. Even if the speaker used local dialect or the audience understood central Thai, respondents often complained that the meetings were so soporific that they were barely awake. And, finally, it is not at all clear that the leadership programs were teaching anything new to their leader students. As we shall discuss shortly, Thai villagers are not necessarily lagging behind the Thai government in understanding the workings of democracy and community action.

These comments should not be read as a blanket denial that training programs have any educational value. Sometimes presentations were said to have raised questions and possibilities that villagers had not considered on their own; and sometimes—though so rarely that we were unable to document a specific instance—subsequent conversations around the village were said to indicate that the lessons of the training session were being remembered and absorbed for future application. But the overall effects of the training programs in changing the way that village leaders operate appeared to be minimal.

Community Development Inputs

The tutorial value of community development inputs is also suspect. As in other developing countries, the Thai government expects the leading benefits of the Community Development Program to include educational ones. Community development is expected to be "an instrument for training the people in self-government and democracy" as the official catechism has it.[1] And, for the immediate need to stimulate local development, it has been taken as self-evident that the native talents of villagers must be bolstered by large doses of education and close supervision from above before they can be applied to the problems of organizing and administering development projects. This belief is reinforced by reports from workers in the field. The village leadership does not do the jobs assigned to it, or is late, or does them wrong, and the official must eventually step in to get the project off dead center.

Accounts of development projects obtained during the research suggest that this may well be true—that once an official takes a hand, the village expects him to make the decisions and to do the supervising. The flaw in concluding from this that the village is incapable of performing these functions for itself is that the official never sees the village when he is not there taking a hand. One of the most striking features of the Thai village is the evidence of organizational sophistication within it.

The evidence emerged in greater detail from four villages selected for an intensive, case-study approach of their development histories. In all, these communities had undertaken 29 community projects since 1960. Some had been initiated and conducted by the village (and are counted as one component of the Civic Investment Index), some had been initiated and conducted by the Thai government. A comparison of the accomplishments of the village and of the government does not indicate how the village was being "taught" anything.

Seven of the 29 projects were planned and implemented without assistance from the government. The seven were comprised of three road projects and construction of two reservoirs, a temple classroom, and a wall around a temple compound. All seven involved substantial problems of planning, design, financing, labor, and special skills. All seven were carried through to completion, and all were "successful," in that they fulfilled the intentions that had inspired them.

Organizationally, the outstanding feature of these projects was the ability of the village leadership to define the component tasks and delegate authority accordingly. In a large project, the division of labor was carried through several levels of authority. The most elaborate example of this was in the construction of the temple classroom. Separate supervisors were selected to head the three main tasks of design and construction, fund-raising, and procurement of materials. Each of these then recruited their own "staffs." The fund-raiser chose three men, and gave them responsibility for collecting donations from a specified section of the village. The construction supervisor selected crew chiefs for the work crews and hired specialized labor for carpentry and masonry. The purchasing supervisor assigned assistants to obtain bids from competitive suppliers. Similarly, the village that built the temple wall selected a specical committee to visit other temples in the district for ideas on design and, during the actual construction, assigned separate supervisors to the jobs of digging clay, manning the kilns, laying bricks, and scheduling shifts (work went on around the clock when the kilns were in use). Moreover, these tasks were generally done methodically. In scheduling shifts, for example, the supervisor would interview each household, determine when each would be most free to contribute labor, convert this information into a written schedule, then return to the household and confirm the shifts that had been assigned to it.

One administrative feature of the temple wall project deserves special note, since it bears directly on the village's capacity to educate itself. This particular village was very poor and could not afford to hire a professional mason to build the entire wall. It could, however, afford a few days of a mason's time. So one was hired specifically to teach a selected villager how to lay bricks. In turn, that villager proceeded to train the rest of his crew.

For less complicated projects the organization of labor was correspondingly simpler. The reservoir and road projects required no specialized labor and very little money, so chiefs for the rotating work crews were all that was needed.

These seven projects gave comparable evidence of an ability to assess village contributions equitably and manage public funds without graft. The rationale for assessing contributions varied depending on the nature of the project. When the project was thought to have equal utility for everyone in the village, all households were asked to make the same donation of time or money. When the project had unequal utility for different people, a sliding schedule of contributions was sometimes used. In the case of the reservoirs, assessments were varied according to how much of the contributor's land would be irrigated. In one of the road projects that required purchases of materials as well as labor, villagers who regularly traded goods at the district market were charged twice as much as villagers who did not.*

Budgeting procedures were familiar to the village leaders at all four sites. A simple written record of income and expenses was kept by the headman and made available for public inspection. This was not a formality. Former headmen in two of the villages had been forced out of office largely because of irregularities in the village finances, and those books that we inspected during the research were detailed, complete with receipts. Disbursement of funds was safeguarded through a system that apparently was standard in all the villages: Money was held in a bank at the district town in the joint name of three men, usually the headman and two others selected by the village. The signatures of all three were required to make a withdrawal. It was a simple system and seemed to work.

Taken overall, the evidence is strongly suggestive of a point that many development managers in Thailand have found hard to accept: Left to themselves, villagers can administer even complex projects competently with no outside help whatsoever. Certainly the organizational skills cannot be directly attributed to government inputs. The four largest and most difficult projects of the seven—the two temple and two reservoir projects—occurred before any sort of government-sponsored community development programs had been introduced. In three of those four cases, the projects antedated virtually any contact with the district office except for routine traditional interactions involving tax collection and registration of landholdings.

Of the 29 projects, 12 were entirely initiated and planned by the district office and provide a clear-cut opposite extreme of government role in village development. They included four "farmers' groups" (of somewhat different types), the building of two schools, a road, an irrigation canal, a fish pond, some privies, the digging of a well, and installation of electricity.

---

*This approach to differential payments was observed in an even more "progressive" form in Chiang Rai province, 600 kilometers away from the four villages that are being described in case studies. Several Chiang Rai villages visited during this study had for many years maintained a standing classification of each household in the village as belonging to one of four economic groups: rich, average, poor, or destitute. The ratings were kept in the headman's books, and whenever the village sponsored a ceremony, festival, or project, costs were varied according to the four groupings. If a villager believed that he had been put in the wrong category, or if his economic situation changed, he appealed to the temple committee for reclassification. The villagers had been doing it for longer than the oldest of the village leaders could remember.

The government's record on these 12 was poor. One of the schools re-placed an existing, adequate building without otherwise changing the quality of education. The other school also replaced an existing school, relocating it at such an inconvenient site that the village fought it all the way to the provincial governor's office. The road went nowhere (literally) as part of a long-range village expansion plan, and uprooted several village houses in its path. The irriga-tion canal became inoperative eight months after its completion. The fish pond had dried up. The well had no water in it for most of the year. Two of the farmers' groups became inactive within a year of being established; the other two were still occasionally being used for purchase of fertilizer. Fewer than 10 per-cent of the villagers used the privies they bought. The single clear success was the electricity project, which did in fact provide electricity.

The remaining ten projects out of the 29 were joint efforts of the village and the government, and the credit for success and blame for failure are corre-spondingly less clear. For our purposes, the point is made by projects at the extremes of village and government control. The histories of them make it extremely unlikely that the tutorial content of the government's community development efforts is producing the correlation betweeen those inputs and the Civic Investment Index.

MANAGED EXPOSURE AND CHARACTERISTICS OF VILLAGE LEADERS

An alternative explanation is that training programs and development inputs have an effect on civic investment when the leaders of the village have the personal abilities to take advantage of them. In this formulation, the inde-pendent variable is the ability of the leader, and the training or development assistance is conceived as playing a facilitative, intensifying role.

A corollary of this hypothesis is that the facilitative role of development inputs are most effective in villages where the more tradition-bound, conserva-tive type of leadership is giving way. Perhaps the new leaders are younger and more flexible. Perhaps the new leaders are merchants or entrepreneurs or others who are showing an aptitude for coping with the moderninzing environment. Whatever the specifics, they are a new generation, and this is intrinsically desir-able for setting villages in motion. This is not a novel viewpoint; something like it is implicit in the attitudes of substantial proportions of Thai development workers and USAID technicians. It was a similar set of expectations that in 1972 prompted the Thai government to apply the mandatory retirement age of 60 to village headmen and hamlet chiefs (kamnan). We generally shared these expecta-tions at the outset of the research.

The logic of the new-generation hypothesis was first jarred by the finding noted earlier that leaders who were engaged in nonagricultural occupations or

who were successfully making money from investments were showing no signs of
being better leaders in community affairs than their noninvesting, rice-farming
counterparts. In fact, it appeared that indirectly their capacity as leaders might
be suffering because of their preoccupations with personal investment.

The expectations were additionally confounded by the finding that as
incidental modernization proceeded, villagers were not choosing younger leaders,
nor were there signs that youth was increasingly valued. Even the assumption
that personal investment behaviors would be more likely to occur among the
younger men rather than among the older (and presumably more conservative)
leaders turned out to be unfounded.

The statistical evidence for these statements is shown in the correlations
below, using two variables about the leader groups: the mean age of members
of a village's leadership group, and tenure, referring to the mean number of
years that members of the leadership group have held an official village position.

	Age	Years in a Village Office
Incidental exposure variables		
Social infrastructure	.09	−.09
Economic infrastructure	.10	.22
Accessibility	.02	−.03
Investment behavior in the village		
Personal Investment Index	.10	−.05
Investment behavior among leaders		
Percentage of village leaders in nonagricultural jobs	−.06	−.02
Noncrop leadership income	−.10	−.12
Behaviors indicating functional capacity		
Civic Investment Index	.06	.40

The table should be read in light of the expectation that these correlations
would be significantly negative. None was. One of them (the .40 correlation
between leader experience and civic investment) was significantly positive.

Qualitatively as well as quantitatively, the relationships we had anticipated
did not materialize. Some of the oldest leaders were among the most enthusiastic and receptive to new ideas. Some leaders who remained subsistence rice
farmers while their neighbors were actively investing turned out to be highly
capable of initiating ambitious community projects. We found no signs that
merchants or other nonfarmers in the village were playing leadership roles as
brokers between the village and the modern outside world that more traditional
leaders were unable to play as effectively. The existence of a new breed of
leader, the young Turk, generational differences in leadership style—this sample
of villages substantiated none of these expectations.

RAISING THE STAKES FOR VILLAGE GOVERNMENT

We return then to the question, Why should community development inputs and training inputs be associated with high levels of civic investment? In particular, why should they appear to be most effective in villages with high levels of incidental exposure to modernizing influences?

The most realistic answer seems to be that managed exposure plays the same role in encouraging functional capacity that incidental exposure plays in encouraging personal modernity. Previously it was argued that the development of accessibility and infrastructure acted to produce both the opportunities and the incentives to invest for personal benefits; now, we are suggesting that community development inputs and training inputs produce the opportunities and incentives to perform leadership roles. They help enrich the content of "being a leader" in a Thai village and keep it competitive with making money.

The explanation is consistent with the pattern shown in Table 6.1, of managed inputs becoming more strongly associated with high levels of civic investment as incidental exposure increases. It is not the isolated villages that need to be taught how to induce civic investment behaviors, but the modernized villages that need to be propped up. The explanation is similarly consistent with the reasons for deterioration in functional capacity presented earlier, when it was argued that village leaders' interest and disinterestedness are undermined by the consequences of personal investment. We are now proposing that managed inputs serve the function of reviving that interest.

Other evidence points to this explanation. It is exemplified by one relatively young member of a village development committee who was designated by the headman to attend a regional conference in a neighboring province. He could remember only the most general contents of the training sessions, but in listening to him discuss the experience with other villagers it became apparent that the conference had meant two important things to him. First, it had been fun, exciting, an outing of grand proportions. Second, as he expressed it to the interviewer, being chosen by the headman as the village's representative had been a signal honor, "because there are others who are older and have much more experience than I." The training conference had been doubly reinforcing regardless of whether it taught him anything. It is plausible to conclude that the conference also made it more likely that he will continue to look upon his development committee membership as worthwhile and important.

The reinforcement value of development assistance was also evident in the responses of village leaders to official recognition of their development work. For example, each district has a "headman of the year" award. It is often given to a headman whose village happened to have been chosen for substantial development assistance that year—because his village thus became the one to show the most conspicuous development progress in that year. It is a circular justification and means that often an undistinguished headman receives the award. But we often observed what seemed to be a self-fulfilling-prophecy effect: The awarded headman showed more activity after receiving the award, in order to maintain the image that he had been given gratuitously. And frequently, conversations with other headmen revealed that their activities were conducted with at least an eye to receiving an official award of merit.

A similar function is served by community development assistance when it generates visits by outsiders to villages with conspicuous development projects. The actual process of doing the project may not have had a spillover effect on the functioning of the village's leaders in other public duties, but it is quite possible that the ceremonial admiration of the Bangkok division chief and the USAID adviser (and maybe even visiting researchers) of the headman, and the comments they leave behind in the ubiquitous visitors' book, do have an effect on the leaders' general level of motivation. Thai villagers are at least as susceptible to praise from status superiors as anyone else, and the input of development assistance vastly increases the likelihood that a village leader will receive that kind of reinforcement.

A final indication that managed exposure succeeds by enriching the content and attractiveness of leader positions emerged from the government's one major attempt to bolster hamlet government, the creation of Council 275, so called after the number of the order establishing it in 1966.

In basic terms, Council 275 put an annual development budget into the hands of a council comprised of headmen and selected villagers, chaired by the kamnan. It replaces the Council 222, which had no regular budget and which was chaired by the chief district officer.

Recent accounts indicate that Council 275 is well designed to achieve its objectives, given proper implementation.[2] But for our purposes, the most pertinent aspects of the program related to the response of village leaders to its initiation. Interviews with village leaders fresh from the three-day training course to introduce the Council 275 in a district of Nakhon Phanom province produced two consistent results: First, the villagers were openly enthusiastic about the idea—in itself, a rare reaction; villagers more commonly will withhold judgment about new government programs. Second, and even more rare, many of the respondents were explicit about what they saw as the main virtue of Council 275: It expanded the scope of local government, and their own roles in it. As one villager put it,

> With the old system [Council 222], members thought it was the district's job rather than the hamlet's, because the meeting could take place only by order of the district office. The meetings were pointless. . . . The new council is the hamlet's responsibility, and the hamlet will do its own work.

Sometimes the confidence of the villagers bordered on cockiness: "I don't want government officers to interfere with the meetings at first," said one headman. "We want to organize our own meetings, and we think we can. Later, if there are any problems, we might ask for some advice." Remembering the otherwise entirely deferential attitude of these same respondents toward the government and its district representatives, their response to the establishment of Council 275 is striking.

Community development inputs and training inputs seldom so clearly change the scope of village leadership (or have a potential for such change, to state it more accurately) as the establishment of Council 275. The explanation we have advanced is very tentatively established by the kinds of indications that are available. But the issue itself is important enough to warrant further exploration. If the statistical relationship of community development inputs and training inputs with civic investment does indeed represent a causal impact on functional capacity of the village, it would more than justify the money spent on those programs. And if it turns out that the mechanism at work is as simple as inspiring villages to do more by giving them more to do, the implications for rural development policy are substantial—as we shall discuss in the concluding section of the study.

NOTES

1. See Arthur H. Niehoff, *A Casebook of Social Change* (Chicago: Aldine, 1966), p. 58. For the Thai case, see Charles A. Murray, *Thai Local Administration: Villager Inter-actions with Community and Amphoe Administration* (Bangkok: U.S. Agency for International Development, 1968), pp. 138ff.

2. See Herbert J. Rubin and Irene S. Rubin, "Effects of Institutional Change upon a Dependency Culture: The Commune Council 275 in Rural Thailand," *Asian Survey* 13 (1973): 240–87.

CHAPTER
7

**IMPLICATIONS FOR A
RURAL DEVELOPMENT STRATEGY**

Throughout the book we have referred tangentially to the implications of the findings for development strategy. In this concluding chapter, we shall try to deal with them directly, grouped under three topics. The first topic is the rationality of villager behavior and its implications for designing local interventions. The next topic deals with the selection and assessment of rural development programs—if economic growth is a priority goal of rural development, what kinds of programs are most likely to succeed? Or should economic growth even be the first order of business in rural development? The final topic deals with an even broader issue: What role can be assigned to the village in the modernization process?

RATIONAL DECISION MAKING AS AN EXPLANATION
OF VILLAGER BEHAVIOR

The development administrator typically comes to his task needing two sets of tools. One set involves the content of a development sector, whether it be agribusiness, preventive medicine, industrial economics, or road engineering. He needs expertise in some specific activity that is to be conducted. The second set of tools involves the people who are the intended beneficiaries of this development; for to be successful, it is almost invariably true that a development input must elicit a behavioral response. People must *use* the new road—or grow the new crop, water their fields from the new irrigation canal, or plow with the new tractor. Good planning and efficient implementation of rural efforts require therefore that the development administrator understand the mainsprings of villager behavior. Along with substantive expertise, he must have the tools to incorporate features into the development project that will make it work in the context of the rural population he is trying to help.

In the process of making these plans, however, the development administrator runs into a major barrier—the visible, tangible differences that separate him from the villager. The anthropological legacy on this subject is especially rich and intricate—it provides detailed accounts of the often radically variant belief systems, economies, social conventions, ceremonies, and eccentricities of major and minor ethnic groups around the world. But the very "other-ness" of villagers that feeds the anthropologist's interest in village life can be an impediment to the development administrator who designs interventions in the village during modernization. The peculiarities and the points of difference tend to deflect simple thinking about why villagers behave as they do.

The deflection is entirely understandable. Villagers *are* different from "us"—meaning modern urban folk—on a variety of dimensions. The development administrator and the villager do in fact live in different material and cultural worlds. The modes of communication across those worlds are not as simple or as efficient as the ones the development administrator can use with his urban neighbor. Communication breaks down, and misunderstandings are frequent—often for no cause that the modern visitor to the village can reasonably ascribe to his own behavior. The "we-they" characterization of the relationship between modernizer and villager that is so often evident in the literature and in the field not only is understandable, but is also in many ways an accurate way to look at the relationship.

Nonetheless, the differences appear to get in the way of the development administrator's perceptions of his job. More specifically, the we-they split in which the "we" stands in such an obviously superior position technologically tends to create in turn a certain condescension when the development administrator tries to assess the reality behind the villager's viewpoint.

The most thoroughgoing form of condescension is the assumption that villagers—peasants—are so different from you and me in their world view, motives, desires, and fears that they are a species apart. They are seen as "benighted," to use the old-fashioned word for it. In this context, the purpose of development is conceived as being to pull them out of their ignorance and squalor to the level of modern folk. It is a twentieth-century version of the "white man's burden." It is also perhaps not as scarce a viewpoint as we would like to believe, even if it is not always put so baldly. Foreign-educated elites in the developing contries often find this view congenial; so do some Americans. The result is a development strategy that does things "for" a rural population. The content of the package and how it is to be delivered are decided through the wisdom in the capital city. The mode of implementation is management by the modernizer with the villagers either wholly uninvolved, or serving as a passive source of labor.

A second, less virulent form of condescension is what might be called mis-directed cultural relativism. The customs and the ethnic peculiaritities of the villagers are "accepted," but with a kind of tolerance more characteristic of a parent's relationship toward a child than the relationship that exists among adults who happen to do things differently. The result is a manipulative approach. The classic example of this occurs when planners attempt to tie the design or implementation of a development project to some local custom. At its best, when applied to basic factors like planting cycles, or traditional organiza-tion of labor, this is a sensible way to approach local implementation. Too often, however, it is applied to religious or purely social customs as a way to circum-vent village resistance. It is tacitly assumed that a cosmetic change will solve the problem. The possibility that the villager's resistance is a function of sound objections that call for a basic redesign (or cancellation) of the project tends to get short shrift.

Perhaps the most common form of condescension is the tendency to pay lip service to the villagers' good qualities. Westerners and often the local govern-ment elites in developing countries delight in rediscovering the "shrewdness" and "common sense" of the villager. In Thailand—other countries undoubtedly have analogous situations—they enjoy the forays upcountry and the evenings spent sipping rice wine with the village elders. They have their favorite headmen, the ones who helped them pull off a successful project, of whom they speak with admiration. But this amiable approach, like the more detached ones, can get in the way of clear thinking about what to do and how to do it in rural develop-ment. For along with the good headmen are the bad headmen who did *not* help pull off the development official's pet project. Along with the pat on the back for the good villager go the lectures and admonitions to the villagers who do not come up to expectations. At the higher administrative levels, these occasional experiences in the field can lead to stereotypes that have no relationship to reality. More insidious, the development administrator in the ministry and the organizer on the ground tend to take on in their own minds the roles of sponsor, protector, and adviser to "their" villagers. It is a paternal relationship. It has the virtues of paternalism, but also the major defect of encouraging a false sense of role and importance by the people on top. A development official can always find evidence that he is needed, that these charming, simple people still are not ready to get along on their own.

Overall, then, an argument can be made that it is easy for development planners, implementors, or evaluators to become excessively conscious of the differences between villagers and themselves. The exotica of the village setting are too distracting from a much simpler proposition, and the one that is advanced here: Villagers generally behave rationally. They are no more rational than the rest of the world—they, like their urbanized counterparts, do strange things on occasion. But it is proposed that typically villagers count costs and risks and benefits as thoroughly as they can with the information at hand, and that their decisions generally make sense. The aspects of village life which are alien to the outsider's way of behaving may obscure the outsider's perception of the calculations at work, but they do not mean that the calculations are not rational ones.

We have touched on this theme at a number of points in the book. We have suggested that the basic social behavioral patterns of villagers in premodern cultures can be explained as a rational response to reality. When a villager is living on the ragged edge of survival in an environment of great scarcity, he is justifiably suspicious of anything that upsets a familiar balance—the more precarious the balance, the more suspicious he is likely to be. When survival is not at issue, in an environment like Thailand's, the villager is more open, and social behavior is more trusting because he has some margin for error, for loss. Despite the wide gap between the social behaviors of a Thai villager and (for example) an Indian one, their behaviors can be seen as sharing a common origin: the reaction of reasonable people to the objective conditions of their environments.

The readiness to adopt innovation draws on the same distinction between scarcity and "sufficiency" village environments. In the scarcity case, we borrow from George Foster's image of limited good to understand the rationality at work:[1]

> Peasant societies are . . . conservative and backward, brakes on national economic progress, [not] because of economic irrationality nor because of the absence of psychological characteristics in adequate quantities. They are conservative because individual progress is seen as—and in the context of the traditional society in fact is—the supreme threat to community stability, and all cultural forms *must* conspire to discourage changes in the status quo. . . . Show the peasant that initiative is profitable, and that it will not be met by negative sanction, and he acquires it in short order.

Decisions to innovate in the sufficiency environment of Thailand were argued to have a parallel rationale. When the extra work involved in taking advantage of free or low-cost resources were not "worth it" in terms of things to do and goods to buy, then aspirations remained delimited. When the incentives started to appear, aspirations started to expand, and so also did behaviors to realize them.

Conspicuous rationality was also described as being evident in the chain of events that make personal investment competitive with civic investment. Villagers who find their contributions to civic goods becoming more expensive will tend to decrease those contributions. Leaders given a choice between opportunities for tangible gains in life quality will pursue them; and as things stand, those opportunities are more salient in the personal setting than in the civic setting.

When it comes to decisions about what to do and how as a community, Thai villagers in the sample villages are argued to have made plans and carried them out with greater efficiency and effectiveness than the government development officials attempting the same kinds of projects. The reason was not that the government officials were lazy or corrupt or stupid, but that the villagers had access to knowledge that the government officials did not have, and took advantage of it in simple but very sensible ways.

Finally, when we addressed the question of why government development and training inputs appear to be effective in sustaining or raising functional capacity, it was again suggested that rational decision-making is at work: Raise the job rewards of being a leader, and villagers are more willing to take on the job.

None of these arguments is intended to convey that villagers are especially virtuous. On the contrary, we contend that they are very ordinary ways for people and communities of people to respond to stimuli. And that is precisely the point: There is less to the we-they distinction in rural development than meets the eye.

The first implication of this view for rural development strategy is simple: The administrator should put himself in the villager's place and ask whether he as a reasonable man would want to grow that new crop or join the cooperative or take that injection given the costs, risks, and benefits involved. The trick, of course, is to make sure that the costs, risks, and benefits are calculated using information and experience available to the villager, not to the administrator.

This points to a second and more important implication: In trying to elicit behavioral response from the village there are sharp limits on what should be done to change the villager's *perceptions* of reality without changing the reality itself. It was common among the development projects in the 41 villages of the sample that villagers chose not to participate in a project because of a lack of trust that the promised benefit would actually occur—that by joining the farmers' group the villager really would be able to buy fertilizer at cut-rate prices, or that the new rice strain would really work in the local soil. It is true that one way to deal with this problem is by changing perceptions. The persuasiveness of the right publicity is undeniable. The difficulty with this solution is that the villager's perceptions are often right to begin with. Governments often do not have a good track record of delivering on promises. Implementation even of the best programs often breaks down at the local level. In this regard, the villager's perception of the odds is likely to be more unflinching than the develpment administrator's; among the villages of the sample, very few respondents had missed out on a good thing by taking a wait-and-see attitude toward programs that relied on government assurances about the future. Perspective can also be a factor. If an administrator can claim success on 80 percent of a certain kind of project, he may have reason for satisfaction. But it may also be that the individual villager cannot tolerate a 20 percent chance of failure.

In short, we are suggesting that when villager resistance to a program exists, do not redouble the publicity and persuasion efforts, but instead take another look at the real risks and the real costs that the program poses from the villager's perspective. Ask whether the answer is to take another whack at his typical peasant obstinacy or to change the substance of the opportunity that is being offered to him.

The assumption that villagers behave rationally is bound to be wrong on some topics in some cultures, as it is sometimes wrong about all populations. It is also true that the rationality is grounded in the specifics of the local situation, and the lessons to be learned from the anthropological and sociological literature can be essential for any given country. Here, we simply argue that explaining villager behavior is easy—or at least easier—once anomalies in villager behavior are assumed to be a reflection of the observer's ignorance of the reality of the village, not a reflection of strange peasant outlooks on reality. For the villagers of this study, "rational decision-making" explained the great bulk of the anomalies, very parsimoniously.

PROGRAMS AND PRIORITIES

Village Economic Development

Increasing villager income is a priority goal, often *the* priority goal, of rural development programs throughout the world. The discussion of "personal investment"—in effect, attempts to increase income—and its apparent causes has an immediate relevance to this objective.

If the villager does indeed react in a fashion that is consistent with the historical scarcity or sufficiency of his environment, then the obvious first step in developing an income-increasing strategy is to ask what kind of environmental model applies to the local situation.

In the real world, of course, very few nations fall into the extremes of scarcity or sufficiency. Most countries fall somewhere in between the poles; often, the environment varies dramatically in different areas within a country. But even if these gradations make it unrealistic to seek for a few "pure" development strategies, planners can at least be warned against taking seriously global generalizations about how the peasant mentality constrains their options. The relevant experiences for a Thai official are those of peasants in parts of Indonesia or Malaysia, or other places with a tradition of independent peasants farming productive land. He can easily be led astray if he tries to learn from the experiences among peasants who have been coping with a hostile natural environment or a feudal tenure system. It is just as dangerous to take the lessons learned by modernizing nations at face value as it is to treat each culture as a unique case. And because "scarcity" nations dominate the picture, it is likely to be the fewer (though more fortunate) sufficiency nations that draw the wrong conclusions from others' development experiences.

Exactly what the differences in strategy ought to be is a question that we can address only partly. The scarcity case is not informed by the data in this study. One may speculate that a patient, tutorial approach to income-raising opportunities is likely to be necessary in the scarcity case. For that villager, penalties for being wrong are so great and the perceived risks so high that the initial resistance to change may be very stubborn.

In the Thai case, however, and for some unknown range of sufficiency environments, the data in this study point to a shift away from community-level economic development efforts and toward general infrastructure development. The data for this study have portrayed a village population that is increasing its entrepreneurial behaviors dramatically, quite possibly at an exponential rate. But these behaviors were not being discernibly affected by the Thai government's income-promoting programs at the village level—a finding that, if it holds true, should have important effects on the budgets of a number of community-level development programs. The logic that is being used to justify substantial expenditures and to tie up some thousands of Thai extension workers finds no support in the data from these villages. Instead, villager behaviors to increase income appear to have followed naturally from additions to rural resources, in the form of roads, dams, irrigation, electrification, health services, police services, and contact with the modernizing outside world. Give the Thai villager exposure to what is available and the opportunities to take advantage of it, and rural economic investment will take care of itself—this was the consistent lesson among the villages in the sample.

Another implied alteration in strategy, and one that is applicable to both the scarcity and sufficiency cases, involves the framework for assessing the success or failure of local economic development programs. The most commonly used measures of program success are what might be called "input verification"— number of bags of fertilizer distributed, number of villages visited by the mobile-development unit, number of village reservoirs built, and so on. For the 41 villages of this study, these measures would have produced an image of a high level of income-raising inputs. Because the ultimate measure of success—a real increase in villager income over time—is exceedingly difficult to measure at the micro level, a common next step in the analysis is to compare the high level of local income-raising inputs with macroeconomic measures of agricultural product. If gross agricultural product is rising (as it is in Thailand), the best guess of the evaluator has to be that a causal relationship is at work. Certainly there are no grounds for claiming that none exists.

The kinds of behavior we classified as "personal investment" indicators provide an intermediate outcome measure for assessing whether that inference is tenable. The use of it has three strengths. The data can be collected inexpensively at the micro level: Data for the six indicators in the index we used could be collected in an hour's visit to a village. The data are objective: Three of the six indicators in our index employed observational data; a fourth can be determined by looking at existing records; none of the six requires a subjective judgment. Most importantly, the data provide a genuine "outcome" measure that tests whether the logic behind the input is being borne out. The same indicators cannot be used interchangeably among countries, but the concept would seem to apply everywhere.[2]

The Question of Priorities

The preceding discussion was based on the assumption that income growth in rural areas is the top priority. But the scarcity/sufficiency issue also raises the question of whether it should be so. Unqeuestionably, an India faced with the prospect of massive food shortages and perhaps famine must think first about economics. But do countries with sufficiency cultures have to make higher villager income their top priority objective in rural development? At least in the Thai case, it is by no means clear that poverty holds first place among the many sectors in which village life is deficient.

Compared to Western standards of living, of course, Thai villagers are poor, and villagers would welcome a higher economic standard of living. But if the question is how village life can *best* be improved, answers other than higher income come to mind. Better health care is one—for every case of malnutrition caused by poverty, how many are caused by ignorance about nutrition? For every infant death caused by poverty, how many are caused by lack of prenatal and postnatal care?

Or if economics are to be given priority, is growth or distribution the more important sector? Two of the great advantages that Thailand brought to the advent of modernization were its high proportion of independent landholders and its low population relative to arable land. A case could be made that Thailand's development resources should be focused not on increasing its rural wealth, but on population control and measures to protect the villager from losing his land. "Way of life" is another potential competitor with economics, though it is seldom perceived as such by development planners. It happens that the Thai people in general, urban and rural alike, believe that they possess certain approaches to life and personal relationships that are superior to other approaches. Among the Thai elite, there is no conscious intention to let modernization destroy these patterns. In view of this, why not treat the nourishment or adaptation of them as a subject to be considered in designing development strategy? It would be an unusual approach for a country to take; it is by no means a nonsensical one.

Other needs in Thailand could be identified that compete with economic growth for attention. Presumably similar examples could be cited in other sufficiency cultures. The point is that although there are few things worse than starving, there are many things worse than being "poor" in the sense that most Thai villagers are poor. The governments of sufficiency cultures, like the governments of other developing countries, do not have the resources to give every problem the attention it deserves. What does set the sufficiency nations apart is the luxury they enjoy of being able to choose priorities on some other basis than the simple physical survival of their populations. In the Thai case, it is a luxury that has not been recognized.

We are not suggesting that a developing nation deliberately avoid economic growth or higher income for villagers. There is no intention of arguing that villagers ought to be guarded from the evils of Western materialism, still less that it would be possible to do so. On the contrary, the evidence suggests that villager efforts to increase income have a life of their own once villager incentives have been activated, regardless of further government encouragement. A pragmatic argument against concentrating rural development resources on economic growth could be made on these grounds alone. Why spend scarce resources to encourage a phenomenon that seems to be accelerating anyway? But that stance misses the more important possibility that, for a country like Thailand, rural economic growth might rank well below the top in a rational list of priorities.

THE USES OF THE VILLAGE

The village is not in favor among development planners. Sometimes it is criticized as being anachronistic, or too small to serve as an effective unit of administration, or too poor in resources. More often, as we discussed at the outset of the book, the village is simply overlooked. Its deficiencies as a tool for modernization are assumed. In contrast to this backdrop are two of the key conclusions of this study: that Thai villages possess or are able to acquire a self-governing capacity that is equal to a wide range of tasks, and that unless something is done about it that capacity will deteriorate as modernization continues.

The underlying question is how the village fits into the structure of the nation-state that each less developed country is struggling to build. Is it assumed that the eventual product will be an urbanized society similar to those of the West? Is the village a unit to be deliberately discarded as soon as possible, or allowed to atrophy as nature takes its course, or deliberately sustained through government policy?

These questions do not permit prescriptive answers; they are among the most intensely individual to each country. In the scarcity case, when something on the order of an amoral-familism moral code has become deeply rooted, it may be futile to try to work through traditional local institutions. Perhaps centralization or reorganization of the countryside is the best approach. But what is characteristic of local government in the scarcity environment is not necessarily true of local government in the sufficiency environment, as the discussion of functional capacity in Thai villages sought to demonstrate. These comments based on the Thai case appear to be in order.

The first conclusion, that Thai villages show a remarkable latent ability to take care of their own affairs, has implications at two levels. On the operational level, it suggests that developing nations look to the possibility of pushing more responsibility out the end of the administrative structure, to the village.

Implementation of small-input local development projects is an obvious use of the village. Too often, village participation in these projects has been justified in terms of its psychological or public relations effects—the common (and patronizing) rationale is that the villagers are more likely to use the input if they feel they have a stake in it. The tendency has therefore been to limit the village's real control over the managerial tasks to cosmetic levels. Symbolic decision-making roles plus the contribution of the village's labor have been thought to be adequate for generating the desired sense of ownership. The data from the sample villages point to the far-reaching possibility that real village *control* is the best way to get the job done right. If we use the most unsentimental of indices—cost control, appropriateness of design, efficiency in implementation and maintenance—the evidence that the village does better than the government on small-input local development deserves much closer examination in the Thai case, and perhaps elsewhere. Even if the village is found to do only "as well" as the government, the possibilities for reducing the existing drain on the government's limited manpower resources are obvious.

But beyond using the village to manage its own projects, developing nations should look more closely at questions about where to locate police powers, juridical authority, tax collection and disbursement, and the other governmental functions that are so widely being arrogated to centralized bureaucracies that are undermanned, underskilled, and too often undermotivated. How long will it be, for example, before the Thai court system can provide the same judicial services to villages that village leaders now provide? More importantly, should it try to do so? Or is it instead desirable to look for ways to adapt and bolster the traditional system already in place?

As we have attempted to show throughout the study, there are good reasons for considering the latter course. What it amounts to is a reevaluation of the proper structural goals for the government of a developing country. Unfortunately, the widespread identification of nationbuilding with the development of centralized and national institutions makes this reevaluation especially difficult. In theory, there is no contradiction between delegating substantial authority to local government and at the same time developing national institutions. But at least among Thai officials and, for that matter, among most scholars in the field of political development, even limited autonomy in the hinterlands is seen as being a hallmark of the premodern state. In historical perspective, that view is correct. It does not mean that centralization of authority is ipso facto modern or desirable. The proposition is that the village is inherently in a better position than the central government to perform certain important tasks of governance, sometimes alone and sometimes in tandem with support services from the district and provincial levels. It is this possibility that makes the prospective deterioration of the village's functional capacity a potentially tragic consequence.

Even on a pragmatic level, the deterioration would be costly. In the Thai case, there were at the beginning of the 1970s some 43,000 villages with some 30 million people living in them. For the foreseeable future, the Thai government will not be ready to take on the burden of the de facto services now provided by those communities to their inhabitants. Insofar as deterioration in functional capacity takes place, those services will go unprovided. And insofar as they are not provived, it will mean fundamental deterioration in the quality of a villager's life for some extended period of time. It is hard to accept that this must be part of a "successful" modernization process. It is even harder to accept in view of the evidence that public policy designed to enrich the content of village government may be effective in halting or even reversing the tendency to deterioration.

This is the pragmatic argument, based on the exigencies facing modernizing governments whose administrative ambitions outreach their current capacity. But perhaps the long-range possibilities for building upon the village as a base should be engaging the attention of development planners. It seems particularly appropriate at this particular point in history that a country like Thailand look to its villages as a continuing focal point for self-government. There is no good reason to acquiesce reflexively in the consolidation of authority at the center at the same time when we in the West are casting about for ways to decentralize units of government that have grown too large and unresponsive, and at the same moment when communications and information technology are creating possibilities for combining centralized resources with local authority.

The developing countries bear a number of costs for modernizing after the West. If there is any advantage in modernizing late, it should be in the possibilities for learning from the West's experience and for traveling on a somewhat straighter course to points that the West is approaching very circuitously. In assessing its village heritage, a developing country should consider whether it is seeing only its society as it has been or also a latent image of what its society might wish to become.

NOTES

1. George M. Foster, "Peasant Society and the Image of Limited Good," *American Anthropologist* 67 (1965): 310. Emphasis added.

2. The use of investment as an indicator of development impact and an application of the theory to the Thai context is described in Robert E. Krug, Paul A. Schwarz, and Suchitra Bhakdi, "Measuring Village Commitment to Development," in *Values in Development: Appraising Asian Experience*, ed. Harold D. Lasswell, Daniel Lerner, and John D. Montgomery (Cambridge: MIT Press, 1976).

APPENDIX A
THE DESIGN AND CONDUCT
OF THE STUDY

This study was carried out in conjunction with a research project conducted by the American Institutes for Research (AIR), a nonprofit research corporation, for the United States Agency for International Development (USAID) and the Royal Thai Government's Agency for Accelerated Rural Development (ARD).

The purpose of the project was to develop methodology for assessing the impact of development programs on Thai villagers and to make that methodology suitable for continuing application by agencies of the Thai government. In practice, this meant the development of criteria for defining positive impact, the development of cheap and relatively simple ways of operationalizing those criteria through data, and, finally, the development of equally cheap and simple ways of monitoring the success of different development programs in achieving those impact criteria.

Part of that final step was to identify conditions within the village—they were called "disposing conditions"—that provide a positive or negative environment for the achievement of development goals. For example, does a rich natural resource base mean that villagers will be eager to take advantage of a new irrigation system; or does their existing prosperity mean that they will have few incentives to use an additional resource? The author had responsibility for conducting the research to examine what these disposing conditions were and how they operated. The results were fully presented in the project reports prepared for USAID and ARD.[1] The sponsoring agencies generously gave the author permission to make the data collection procedures compatible with the closely related objectives of this study, to examine what this writer perceived as significant variance in the quality of life among Thai villages.

THE SAMPLE

The study was conducted in district Thoeng of Chiang Rai province in the far north of Thailand; district Lomsak in Petchabun province of north-central Thailand; district Amnatcharoen of Ubiol province in northeastern Thailand; and districts Mukdahan, That Phanom, and Tha Uthen of Nakhon Phanom province, also in the Northeast.

The villages included in the study were drawn from two previous samples. All but four of them were drawn from a sample of 129 villages covered during an earlier survey by the AIR impact assessment project. Those 129 villages had been chosen randomly within three strata: within one kilometer of an all-weather road, within five kilometers of an all-weather road, more than five kilometers from an all-weather road. The number of villages selected from each stratum had been made proportional to the distribution of the overall village population in the district: If 50 percent of the villages in district X were within one kilometer of an all-weather road, 50 percent of the sample for that district was chosen from among those villages. In all, the 129 villages represented a 25 percent sample of the population of villages in the four districts of that study.

The extra four villages included in the sample for this study, but not included in the previous AIR study, were communities in which the author had previously conducted extensive residence research, with two researchers resident in each village for a month.[2] Because these four villages came from a district of Nakhon Phanom province (one of the provinces included in the AIR survey), and because they also represented a range of levels of accessibility to an all-weather road, it was considered that they would be compatible with the rest of the sample. Their addition brought the substantial benefit of allowing a new look at villages examined almost five years earlier—in two cases, by one of the same researchers who had participated in the residence research at that time.

Data were collected from a total of 49 villages that are carried on the Thai government's books as distinct administrative entities. The realities of the situation led us to collapse this number to the 41 that comprise the base for virtually all of the analyses. In one instance, five villages were effectively administered by a single headman; in four other instances, pairs of contiguous villages were treated as one.

The 41-village subset was a remarkably faithful reflection of the parent sample. Means of some representative variables are shown in Table A.1.

Three of the most important village parameters are not included in the table. They are distance from the district town, number of households, and regional location. Some observations about the representativeness of the sample on each of these dimensions are worth noting in more detail.

The distances of the 41 villages from their respective district towns appear to be highly representative of the general population of villages in North and Northeast Thailand. The basis for this statement is a map exercise conducted with a randomly chosen sample of 300 villages in 15 provinces from those regions. After we deleted those "villages" that turned out to be located within the municipal boundaries of the district towns, a sample of 272 villages remained. The mean distance of these villages from their district towns was 17 kilometers; the mean distance for the 41-village sample was 16.7 kilometers. The details of the distribution are shown in Figure A.1.

Table A.1
Comparison of Means on Representative Variables in the 129-Village and 41-Village Samples

Variable	129-village sample	41-village sample
Age, head of household	44.7	44.7
Number of *rai* owned per household *	22.1	22.1
Percentage of households selling produce	73.6	75.7
Percentage of households using fertilizer	42.2	42.4
Percentage of households using insecticide	40.0	41.4
Number of stores per 100 households	2.4	2.5
Number of rice mills per 100 households	1.2	1.5

* One *rai* is equal to approximately .4 acres.

As Figure A.1 shows, the shape of the 41-village sample closely conformed to the shape of the larger sample.

The villages in the 41-village sample ranged in size from 54 to 575 households. The mean was 145.4 households compared to 123.0 for the 129-village sample. The 41-village sample is probably more unrepresentative on this parameter than on any other. The very small villages of 20, 30, or 40 households were not represented at all, and it is probable that the sample for this study has a disproportionately large number of villages in the 100-to-200-household range.

Figure A.1

Representativeness of the Sample in Distance from the District Capital

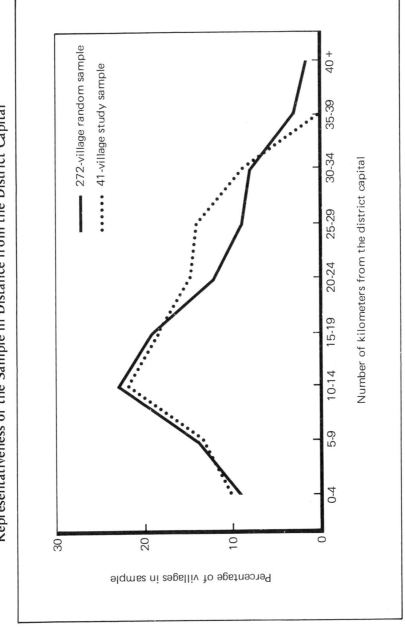

Figure A.2

Representativeness of the Sample
in Number of Households per Village

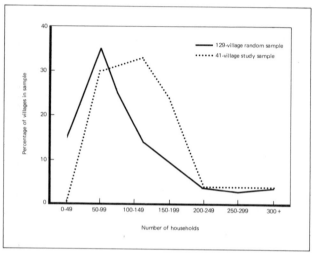

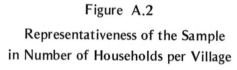

See the comparison of the size distributions in the 41-village and 129-village samples, as shown in Figure A.2.

The underrepresentation of the very small village was intentional. Previous AIR surveys had indicated relatively high correlations between village size and a number of the variables of interest to this study, even when the scoring expressed variables in terms of percent of population or percent of households.[3] It was felt that this reflected the importance of attaining a "critical mass" in village size more than a direct linear relationship between village size and the responses to modernization that are examined in this study; and, in fact, village size proved to be insignificantly correlated with those responses when the sample was truncated to exclude villages of less than 50 households. This means, however, that the findings of this study are not to be associated with the roughly 15 percent of villages in the provinces of the study that fell into that category.

With the exception just noted, there is no reason to believe that the 41 villages of this sample are systematically unrepresentative of the overall population of villages in the North and Northeast. On the contrary, the available evidence suggests that they were unusually representative of the parent 129-village sample and, in view of the stratified random sample employed in selecting it, representative of the general population.

This is not to claim that the 41 villages are representative of all Thai villages; the question of regional differences remains. The Central Plains and the South present peculiar features that may make some or all of the findings inapplicable to them. In particular, the much longer exposure of the villages of the Central Plains to the influence of modernization probably means that a survey of that region would yield substantially different results. The differences might indicate simply that the Central Plains villages are Northern and Northeastern villages 30 years from now. But in the absence of data, the question remains open.

This procedure would be especially suspect if the data from the North included information from the hill tribe villages, which have a cultural heritage clearly incomparable to that of the lowland Thai. But hill tribe villages were not included in the survey, and it has been assumed that the cultural differences among the various ethnic subgroups in North and Northeast villages are not significant for an analysis of the variables in this study.

Even though that statement might pain an anthropologist—the ethnic variegation of Thai villages is rich and intricate—the data give no indication that interregional differences on any of the variables are best explained by appeals to inherent differences in culture or ethnicity. That is, it so happens that the North and Northeast are different in their economic environments as well as in their historical and ethnic environments. Not surprisingly, then, analyses of variance using regional groupings often yield significant differences in behaviors related to economic conditions. But when (as proved to be the case in this study) the relatively few poor villages in the North behaved similarly to the many poor villages in the Northeast, it seems reasonable to assume that the source of difference in economic-related behaviors is the village's economic environment, not a regional culture.

THE FIELD RESEARCH
The Personnel

The field research team was comprised of five people. Three of them—Messrs. Suthat Khlangsuphan, Sivasak Seubsaeng, and Chaiyasit Hotorakit—were Thai field interviewers seconded to the project from the Agency for Accelerated Rural Development (ARD). The fourth member of the team, Mr. Pholachart Kraiboon, was a Thai researcher employed by AIR throughout the impact assessment project. The author was the fifth member of the team and directed the design and conduct of the research.

The Field Research Schedule

The data were collected during the period of August 1972 to February 1973 in a series of five field trips. This was a residence research study, with the field interviewers living in the village full-time. The length of stay in each village (one interviewer per village) was approximately six days, with some exceptions according to specific circumstances. The writer rotated his visits among all the villages of the sample.

Data were collected from three major sources: interviews with village leaders, structured observation, and interactions with the general village population. Data collection procedures for each of these sources are discussed below.

Interviews with Village Leaders

The first task of the field interviewer was to identify the members of the leadership group in the village. To do so, he would ask the headman to name the people who were especially respected by the villagers, whose advice was sought most often, and who were most active in guiding village affairs. When the headman was satisfied that he understood the question, he would name all those villagers whom he considered to be leaders. Subsequently all of the people named were interviewed in turn, and asked the same question: Who are the leaders in this village? The process continued until no new names were forthcoming, and all the people named had been interviewed.

Certain categories of villager were automatically included as respondents, regardless of whether they were nominated as leaders. These categories included the headman, assistant headmen, kamnan (hamlet chief) when he lived in the village being studied, village merchants, and the school's headmaster. But the population of leaders used for data-analysis purposes did not include these persons unless they had been named by villagers as actual as well as putative leaders. Specifically, a person was said to be a leader (for data analysis) if he was nominated at least twice, or by more than 10 percent of the sample in that village, whichever was greater.

Interviewers questioned randomly selected villagers about the leadership group in order to guard against the possibility of getting only a clique from the leader self-nomination procedure. For data collection purposes, a person was given the full leader interview if he was mentioned even once.

The basic leader interview included the following elements: elementary biographical data; personal economic data about possessions and occupation; data on his education and training, on his children, if any, on leadership functions, problems, and satisfactions, on his evaluations of other leaders; and a set of critical incidents about his involvement in development projects, other administrative and adjudicative acts (formal or otherwise), transmission of information or advice, and personal investments in self-improvement.

Interviews with the headman and Kamnan included an additional set of questions. These covered the frequency of, and examples of, 13 leadership-related behaviors. As a matter of course, the interviews with headmen and kamnan were more extended and more detailed than those with other leaders.

Table A.2
The Leader Interview Sample

Position	Number	Percent
Kamnan (hamlet chief)	10	1.9
Headmen	41	8.2
Assistant headmen or *kamnan*	85	16.9
Heads of committee	54	10.7
Committee members	228	45.3
Other	85	16.9
TOTAL	503	99.9

The interviewer was also instructed to obtain a variety of facts and information about the village, using the most knowledgeable available source when observation was not feasible. These categories were included: water resources for agriculture, water resources for household use, soil quality, topography, local crops and extent of production, cottage industries, other nonagricultural occupations, educational facilities, other skills resources (such as army veterans with skills), stores, rice mills, tractors, and other economic resources, police and security forces in the vicinity, insurgent activity in the vicinity, local religious characteristics, local ethnic and interfamily characteristics, health facilities in the vicinity, and transportation and communications resources.

The basic interview usually took more than one session to complete thoroughly. The total time per respondent varied widely, depending on both the extent of the respondent's activities and the interviewer's inclination. A rough average is about two hours for the sample as a whole, and four to five hours for the two or three primary leaders in a community. In all, 503 full-scale interviews were completed, as shown in Table A.2.

The interview techniques employed were a combination of the focused interview and the critical incident techniques.[4] Both methods have in common a conversational flexible format that we believe to be appropriate to the interview environment of a Thai village. The critical incident technique in particular has proved useful in opening up respondents who are apprehensive. It in effect asks the respondent to recount a story about the "last time" that he found himself in a specific type of situation—asked to settle a dispute or asked to participate in a development project, to take two examples from the interview forms. Narratives are very much in the Thai village tradition, and the critical incident format appeared to provide a congenial way for the villager to express himself.

The weakness of the focused interview and critical incident techniques is a low level of standardization in the raw data. This, however, is crippling primarily if the analysis entails quantitative attitudinal topics. When the data to be quantified are exclusively of factual content, standardization can more easily be imposed during the data analysis phase of the study. And as an examination of the variables actually used in the quantitative analysis will indicate (see Table A.3), the data points quantified from interview responses had very little subjective content.

The Observational Survey

Observational data played a major role in the field study. All of the observations in all of the villages were carried out by the author, both to maximize the internal consistency of the scaled items and to guarantee the validity of the observations.

The core of the observational survey was a house-by-house examination of the village. It was close to complete. Out of the 5,954 houses reported to be in the sample villages, 5,198 were examined and rated—87.3 percent. A detailed description of the data points is given in the section on data analysis, below.

Several other observational data were systematically collected. The condition of the temple(s) in the village, the school, the village streets, and other public facilities were all rated. Development inputs reported by the village leaders were inspected, when applicable. An inventory was taken of the goods for sale in the village's stores. A complete map of the village was made as a by-product of the house-by-house survey.

Informal Interactions with the Village Population

One of the principal advantages of residence research is the opportunity it affords for unstructured interviews, observations, and group discussions. The researchers were instructed to seek out these targets of opportunity. The author, who did not conduct the "official" interview with village leaders, spent many hours in casual interaction with villagers at each site. These encounters yielded substantial information about factors in the community such as long-standing feuds among families, stories of competing interests, networks of friends, spontaneous expressions of opinion about local and government leadership, and a variety of other types of anecdotal data that were useful both for developing a sense of the social environment of the village, and in evaluating the significance of the more structured data. The number of these contacts ran well into the hundreds. No attempt was made to formalize or count them.

DATA ANALYSIS

Scoring the Variables

The analysis moves between a discussion of the qualitative aspects of Thai village life and the quantitative variables that are said to operationalize them. Twenty-six of these quantitative variables are used in the analysis, and they cover a broad spectrum of types. The label of each variable, its content, and the metric in which it is expressed are shown in Table A.3. Scoring procedures for variables with artificial metrics are explained in the following discussion.

In addition to the 26 variables in Table A.3, two indexes are employed to represent the central constructs of the study, personal and civic investment. The indicators used in the indexes are drawn from the 26 variables in Table A.3, and are discussed at length in Chapters 2 and 4. The index scores themselves are a sum of the standardized scores of the individual indicators. A standardized score is the distance of a given observation from the mean of the distribution, expressed in standard deviations:

$$z = \frac{x - m}{s},$$

where z is the standardized score, x is a raw score, m is the mean of the distribution, and x is the standard deviation of the distribution.

In effect, then, the indexes express the "unusualness" of a village on the construct rather than its place on an anchored scale. The rationale for the procedure was that in adding apples and oranges, as these indexes do (for example, number of stores plus percentage of households growing cash crops), standardized scores have the virtue of providing a common metric for the indicators, and one that is widely familiar. The other main alternative, to assign arbitrary weights to the different units (for example, one store is given the same weight as 20 percent of households growing cash crops), was intrinsically less attractive on this count alone.

An additional reason for using standardized scores is that there is no a priori definition of what comprises "many stores" in a village or "many cash crop farmers" (to continue with the same examples). Given a sample of villages that is reasonably representative of a population, and given that the parent population contains a range from "very few" to "very many" on the variables of interest, standardized scores provide natural weights that are informative and appropriate when the intention is to measure differences among villages rather than to assign them absolute scores.

Table A.3
Summary of the Quantitative Variables Used in the Study

CONTENT	METRIC
• Cultivation of cash crops	Percentage of households (hh)
• Commercial vehicle ownership	Number in village per 100hh
• Rice mill ownership	Number in village per 100hh
• Store ownership	Number in village per 100hh
• Persons in nonagricultural employment	Number in village per 100hh
• Membership in credit cooperatives	Ordinal scale *
• Accessibility to the outside world	Ordinal scale *
• Economic infrastructure near the village	Ordinal scale *
• Social infrastructure near the village	Number of facilities *
• Community development assistance from the government during the last five years	*Baht* equivalent
• Training courses attended by village leaders	Mean number among leaders
• Land and water resources	Ordinal scale *
• Upkeep of house compounds	Percentage of houses rated 5 or more on ordinal scale *
• Extent and upkeep of internal village streets	Ordinal scale *
• Upkeep of the village's temple(s)	Ordinal scale *
• Village-initiated development projects during the last five years	Number
• Leaders whose main income is from nonagricultural sources	Percentage of leaders
• Leader income derived from non-crop sources	Mean annual *baht* among leaders *
• Age of village leaders	Mean age in years
• Experience in official positions	Mean no. of years among leaders
• Intra-village economic disparity in housing	S.D. of combined size and expense ratings *
• Substandard village housing	Percentage of houses with size and expense 3 or less on 9-point ordinal scale *
• Superior village housing	Percentage of houses with size and expense 7 or more on 9-point ordinal scale *
• Evidence of demoralization among the bottom income group in a village	Percentage of substandard houses rated 3 or less on upkeep of compound *
• Magnitude of the landholding gap between leaders and village	Standardized expression of differences in means *
• Percentage of leaders in a landholding elite	Percentage of leaders with landholdings above average

* *An explanation of the scoring system is given in the text.*

Calculation of Standardized Scores for
Variables Using Ordinal Measures

The indexes for this study were constructed by summing standardized scores on the separate indicators. This raises the following question: How are standardized scores to be obtained for variables measured at the ordinal level? One possibility is to express the values of the variable in terms of an arbitrarily chosen interval scale (unit increments is the obvious choice), then proceed to calculate the mean, standard deviation, and standardized scores as if the data had been measured at the interval level in the first place. A second possibility, and the one used for this study, is to use a normalizing technique.

In effect, the normalizing technique assigns a z-score, which represents the average distance of any given category of an ordinal variable from the center of the distribution, under a normal curve.[5] It boils down to four steps: (1) calculate the percentage of the sample in each category, array in order, and assume a normal curve; (2) look up the ordinates of the normal curve at the dividing points between the categories; (3) for any given category, subtract the righthand ordinate from the lefthand ordinate; and (4) divide the difference by the proportion of the sample in that category. The result is the mean deviation of a portion of a unit normal distribution and is the score to be assigned to all cases that fall in the category in question. The procedure has the advantage of allowing the calculation of a standardized score by using the single assumption of normality; it does not require the analyst to impose arbitrary metrics on the original categories.

With this general procedure in mind, we will turn to explanations of the variables starred in Table A.3.

Level of Substandard Housing, Level of Superior Housing,
and Intravillage Economic Disparity in Housing

All three of these variables were based on the house-by-house survey and are most easily explained together. Each house was scored on three items: size, expense of materials used in the house, and condition of the compound surrounding the house.

Size of the house was scored on a nine-point scale ranging from a tiny porchless hut for "1" to a large, multiroom house with a large porch for "9." Describing the intermediate scores requires a background in Thai village architecture. Roughly, an increment of one point meant an increment of size equivalent to half of a typical motel room, with "5" denoting a house of about two motel rooms in size, plus a porch on stilts above a usable open space beneath.

Expense of materials used in building the house was also scored on a nine-point scale, with the intervals delimited as follows: (1) leaf walls and a thatch roof; (2) leaf walls and a tin or tile roof, or mat walls and a thatch roof; (3) mat walls and a tin or tile roof; (4) some wood used in the walls and a tin or tile roof, or solid wood with a thatch roof; (5) solid wood with a tin or tile roof; (6) same as "5", with evidence of skilled carpentry and fittings; (7) a cabinet house: skilled carpentry throughout; (8) same as "7" plus a substantial additional expense such as lower wall made of masonry; (9) a house made entirely of masonry.

Condition of the compound, like size of the house, was an objective rating that is nonetheless difficult to describe short of photographs to illustrate the gradations. A "5" meant a clean, neat compound with no frills at all; the higher and lower numbers work out from both directions to "1" (given only to four houses out of the 5,198), denoting piles of debris and unrelieved filth, and to "9," denoting the Thai village equivalent of a compound ready to be photographed by *Better Homes and Gardens*. It was taken to be crucial to the validity of the measure that the rating not be affected by adornments that cost money. The smallest shack was eligible for a "9" rating on condition. It was a measure of expenditure of care and pride, not money.

It was found, as is usually the case with judgmental rating systems, that some experience was required before the judgments stabilized. What was thought to be a "2" in size during the survey of the first village was being treated as a "3" by the time the third village was reached. In order to guard against distortions in the intervillage comparisons, the ratings for the first four villages were discarded, and those villages were rescored during a return visit to that province shortly before the field research was completed. These four villages had included 829 house ratings; in effect, those ratings were for practice. Although no reliability tests were possible (in the absence of another trained rater to cover some of the same villages independently), the generous number of "warm-up" ratings gives some reason to be confident that a stable internal conception of the meaning of the scale values was applied throughout the sample. Added to that is the subjective perception of the rater that, after the first few hundred cases, there was seldom any hesitation about the ratings to assign a given house.

Evidence of Low-Income Group Demoralization

This variable also was based on the house-by-house survey, combining the ratings of conspicuously poor maintenance with signs of conspicuously low income. The use and scoring of the variable are described in the body of the book (Chapter 5). This variable is treated as mathematically independent from the Civic Investment Index, despite the fact that both draw (in some fashion) on the "upkeep of house compounds" variable. Some justification of this procedure is appropriate.

The confounding involves the "upkeep of house compounds" variable (YARDS, for convenience) used in the Civic Investment Index and the demoralization variable (SLUM). Three data points are involved: size of the house (SIZE), expense of materials of the house (EXPENSE), and the condition of the house compound (CONDITION). Now, consider the algorithm for the two variables, SLUM and YARDS:

$$\text{SLUM} = \frac{\text{no. of houses with SIZE} \leqslant 3 \text{ and EXPENSE} \leqslant 3 \text{ and CONDITION} \leqslant 3}{\text{no. of houses with SIZE} \leqslant 3 \text{ and EXPENSE} \leqslant 3}$$

$$\text{YARDS} = \frac{\text{no. of houses with CONDITION} \geqslant 5}{\text{total no. of houses surveyed}}$$

which we shall abbreviate in set notation as follows:

$$\text{SLUM} = \frac{S \cap E \cap C_1}{S \cap E}$$

$$\text{YARDS} = \frac{C_2}{H}$$

The two constraints on these sets are that

$$S, E, C_1, C_2 \supset H \qquad \text{and}$$

$$C_1 \cap C_2 = \phi$$

This translates into the following: If all the houses in the village are rated 5 or higher on CONDITION, YARDS equals unity and SLUM must equal zero. If none of the houses is rated 3 or lower on CONDITION, we know that SLUM equals zero (we do not know the value of YARDS, because of houses that may have been rated 4). If none of the houses in the village was rated 3 or less on both SIZE and EXPENSE, SLUM has no value. The key point is this: If any houses are rated 3 or less on condition, the range of values for SLUM is not constrained by the value of YARDS, even though the size of the intervals is constrained. For example, if in a village of 100 households, 98 are rated 5 or higher on CONDITION, then obviously SLUM must be one of three values: 0, .50, or 1.00. But then knowing that 98 of the households are rated 5 or higher on CONDITION or that YARDS equals .98 gives us no clue about which of those three values SLUM will take. In the event, every village in the sample had houses rated 3 or lower on CONDITION and houses that were rated 3 or lower on both SIZE and EXPENSE: hence the conclusion that SLUM and YARDS appear to be wholly unconfounded for this data set.

We may add another consideration. SLUM was correlated with the other three indicators in the Civic Investment Index at -.43. So even if mathematical confounding between SLUM and YARDS could be demonstrated, it would not materially affect the conclusions drawn in the text based on the -.61 correlation between SLUM and the full Civic Investment Index.

Membership in Agricultural Credit Cooperatives

The three-point scale is (1) no cooperatives in the village; (2) less than 20 members (attrition in membership); and (3) 20 members or more.

The reason for not treating membership continuously is that co-ops are established in 20-member groups. No fourth category for villages with more than one group is given, because of substantial differences in policy on more than one group per village among banks in the different districts of the sample. Standardized scores on the variable were obtained through the normalizing procedure.

Accessibility to the Outside World

The accessibility variable is generated by scoring villages twice on each of two four-valued dimensions, as follows: "Accessibility to what": (1) large province town (for sample, Ubol, Chiang Rai, Nakohn Phanom); (2) large district town or small province town (Lomsak, Mukdahan, That Phanom, Petchabun); (3) average district town (Amnatcharoen); (4) small district town (Thoeng, Tha Uthen). "Difficulty of access for a villager": (1) a trip to town takes just a few minutes in addition to the time spent on business, any time of day; (2) a trip to town usually means losing half of the work day; (3) a trip to town usually means losing most of the work day; (4) a trip to town means losing the entire work day.

Each village is scored on "difficulty of access" for both the district and province towns nearest it. For this sample, the procedure created no anomalies (for example, a village in one district that is very close to the town of a neighboring district).

It was assumed that "difficulty of access" is a more important consideration than the gradations of the size of the towns. On the basis of this assumption, a matrix scaling procedure was completed (see illustration below) by entering each village twice, according to its accessibility to the district and

	Large province	Large district	Average district	Small district
A few minutes		V_1 V_2	V_3 V_4	
Half-day	V_1 V_5	V_5		
Most of day	V_2 V_3 V_4			
All day				

The ordering: $V_1 > V_2 > (V_3, V_4) > V_5$ in accessibility.

province towns. Thus, the scorer starts at the top row of the matrix and works through every village which is only "a few minutes" away from somewhere. All of those villages will be ranked higher on accessibility than villages that are no closer than a half-day away from the district and province towns, no matter whether they are larger than the equivalent towns for the higher-rated villages.

Some ties occur when two or more villages are identically distant from identical types of towns (for example, v_3 and v_4 in the illustration). In the case of the 41 villages of the sample, the result was a set of 20 ordered levels of accessibility.

Economic Infrastructure near the Village

Economic infrastructure is assumed to consist of two types: agricultural, meaning large-scale irrigation systems, flood control systems, or other facilites beyond the village's capacity to build; and nonagricultural, referring to factories or other employers near enough to be a viable source of employment for villagers. In the case of agricultural infrastructure, a negative value was also defined: some feature of the topography or general environment (besides poor soil or lack of water) that clearly constrained agricultural activity—for example, frequent flooding from a nearby river. Normalized scores were obtained for the three-valued agricultural infrastructure item and the two-valued nonagricultural infrastructure item, and summed to form the economic infrastructure measure.

Social Infrastructure in the Village

The following facilities were counted: school beyond the fourth grade, health center, movie theater, community center, electricity, and police post. A school to the fourth grade only and a temple were treated as standard facilities, and not counted.

Land and Water Resources of the Village

Only rough estimates of soil fertility were possible. Available data on land productivity are untrustworthy, and it was decided to assign only "conspicuously fertile" or "conspicuously barren" to unusual cases, based on a variety of estimates—from the Thai government's agriculture agencies, the villagers, and economic statistics in the archives. Water resources were gradated equally simply, carefully excluding changes in water resources that the village might have effected by its own efforts (in order to make sure that this variable was legitimately treated as exogenous). The negative value for water resources was "no nearby river." The neutral value was nearby wet-season river," and the positive value was "nearby year-round river." Normalized standard scores for the two trichotomous items were summed to form the variable.

Upkeep of House Compounds

The nine-point scale for grading house compounds was described earlier. The percent of houses with a rating of "5" (clean, but no frills) or higher was chosen as the measure for this variable, to give extra weight to low variance within a village. Simply using the mean on the compound rating would give high scores to villages with extremes of good and poor upkeep. The object of the measure, as discussed in Chapter 4, is to identify the degree to which a village as a whole exhibits evidence of high morale and, for want of a better phrase, community spirit.

Extent and Upkeep of Internal Village Streets

The key factor is not whether village houses are directly on a village street. Often a house will be within 20 or 30 meters of a street and yet have as complete access as a house fronting on it. Or, in other cases, the streets are so poorly maintained that even the houses directly on the street cannot use it except during the dry season. To get around these problems, a village's street system was assessed on two dimensions, as follows:

"Households cut off from access to a street of any kind": (1) none (0 percent); (2) a small cluster (1–10 percent); (3) a major cluster (11–50 percent); (4) most of the village (more than 50 percent).

"Extent of the village street-building and maintenance effort": (1) major system of village-built and maintained streets; (2) some village-built streets and/or well-maintained government road through the village; (3) no evidence of village efforts to build and/or maintain internal streets.

The two dimensions were combined on the assumption that the number of people cut off from a road is more important than the extent of the village's effort, leading to a 12-point fully ordered scale. For purposes of combining the variable with the other indicators of civic investment behavior, the normalizing procedure was applied to the scale values.

Upkeep of the Village's Temple

A simple three-point scale was used: conspicuously inferior maintenance of the temple compound and building; average maintenance; conspicuously superior maintenance. It was assumed that the negative inferences to be drawn from an unkempt temple are more reliable than the positive inferences from a good one (which may be a product of initiatives taken by just a few people in the village). So whereas the first two categories were rated from observation alone, assignment to the "superior" category required corroborative evidence from other sources that unusually high villagewide effort was being put into upkeep of the temple. The normalizing procedure was applied to the ratings.

Leader Income Derived from Noncrop Sources

The figure was estimated from leader self-reports on assets and income, plus evidence from observational sources and other interviews. Two facilitating Thai-specific factors should be noted. First, personal income is not the private matter in Thailand that it is in the United States. In social conversation, asking someone what he makes is entirely acceptable. Second, the villagers were not likely to avoid answering accurately out of fear of taxes, because taxes are not collected for the levels of income reached by any but a few of the respondents, because taxes are not often collected in villages for the handful of villagers who did have taxable levels, and because of precautions on our part to be clearly identified as what we were: interviewers for a project sponsored by ARD and USAID.

Magnitude of the Economic Gap Between Leaders and Nonleaders

A more complete discussion of the scoring for this variable is included in the text and notes of Chapter 5, because understanding how it was scored is necessary to understanding what the variable means. Briefly, this variable is a proxy z-score, whereby the mean landholdings of the leader group are expressed in terms of distance from the mean of landholdings of a random sample of villagers.

THE USE OF PATH ANALYSIS

Statements of causation are discussed in conjunction with regression and one of its special applications, path analysis.[6] The application of these techniques is restrained, as befits a sample of 41 observations and a subject matter that is very imperfectly operationalized through quantitative statements. This restraint shows up in two respects.

First, the model deals only with one-way causal relationships. The two-stage least-squares method for estimating reciprocal relations was considered but has not been used.[7] The mathematical constraint it imposes on a model (that is, the identification requirement) was not satisfactorily reconciled with the even more important requirement that the model's exogenous variables reflect the realities of rural Thailand. The coefficients that the two-stage least-squares method produces, although consistent and unbiased in their mathematical properties, are nonetheless reflective of fitted values of the causal variables. This can create misunderstandings when the first stage of the regression has left substantial variance unexplained and, consequently, substantial error terms. Most importantly, the crucial relationships in the theoretical model are either genuinely one-way or, in a few cases, so overwhelmingly one-way from the theoretical perspective that the feedback loop could be assumed to be of negligible importance. For all these reasons, the simpler unidirectional model was judged to be appropriate to this study.

Second, the study does not seek to develop the path model that most perfectly conforms to the mathematical desiderata of the technique. One of the principal attractions of the path model is the existence of prediction equations for unconnected variables: if X and Y are unrelated causally, the bivariate correlation between X and Y should equal the sum of the causal paths that connect the two variables indirectly. More formally, the algebra of path analysis leads to the basic theorem that

$$r_{ij} = \sum_q p_{iq} r_{jq}$$

where i and j denote two variables in the system and the index q runs over all variables from which paths lead directly to the ith variable.[8]

The existence of this test for causally unrelated variables poses this problem: When the expected result does not occur, does one change the model? Is the reader to be presented with a model that has gone through numerous iterations until the prediction equations lead to minimized mathematical discrepancies, or is the original theory with only minor modifications tested through path analysis, and the discrepancies left untreated?

Given a small sample and the inevitable degree of epistemic error that must characterize the variables we have measured, the latter option seems much more sensible. This is not to say that the causal chain was carried full-blown into the data collection, waiting only for the numbers to be plugged in. On the contrary, there was an interaction between theory construction and data throughout the process. But the formal application of the data to the tests of path analysis came late in the game, and only the most elementary changes were made as a result of those tests.

The general stance we have taken toward path analysis is this: A theory has been developed on the basis of a wide range of inputs about how modernization works in rural Thailand. When some of the most important causal links were tested through path analysis, the theory was supported in some respects, not supported in others. Still other aspects of the results suggest changes and amplifications of the model. These findings are all reported. But the correlations and path coefficients from the villages of the sample are neither so stable nor so representative that they justify the rejection of links supported by other data (or common sense), or adding links not consistent with the other data.

The approach to quantitative analysis in this study was that it could inform and often clarify the overall analysis. It is thought to provide important evidence in support of the major contentions of the argument. But the quantitative aspects of the study have not in any way dominated the qualitative ones. On the contrary, there is a need to treat qualitative perceptions and quantitative forms of analysis as equal partners, and to let the strengths of one step in for the weaknesses of the other—with the proviso that the decisions on what to quantify, how to quantify it, and what manipulations to perform on the quantity should flow from an initial qualitative familiarity with the terrain of the research—in this case, the Thai village.

NOTES

1. The principal related reports were Charles A. Murray, *Village-Level Disposing Conditions for Development Impact* (Bangkok: American Institutes for Research, 1973), and Robert E. Krug and Steven M. Jung, *Systems for Evaluating the Impact of Rural Development Programs* (Bangkok: American Institutes for Research, 1974.

2. Charles A. Murray, *Thai Local Administration: Villager Interactions with Community and Amphoe Administration* (Bangkok: United States Agency for International Development, 1968).

3. See Robert E. Krug, *Some Evaluations of ARD Program Impact in Four Amphoe* (Bangkok: American Institutes for Research, 1972).

4. The basic sources are Robert K. Merton and Patricia L. Kendall, "The Focused Interview," *American Journal of Sociology* 51 (1946): 541–57; and John C. Flanagan, "The Critical Incident Technique," *Psychological Bulletin* 51 (1954): 327–58.

5. The procedure is fully described in Truman Lee Kelley, *Fundamentals of Statistics* (Cambridge: Harvard University Press, 1947), pp. 295–97.

6. The acceptance of path analysis as a tool for social scientists is expanding to the point that an explanatory note is almost unnecessary. Path analysis has a long history in the physical sciences, particularly genetics, dating back to Seward Wright's "Correlation and Causation," *Journal of Agricultural Research* 20 (1921): 557–85. Much of the impetus for

its use in sociology and political science derives from the work of Herbert A. Simon and H. M. Blalock, Jr. (for example, Simon, "Spurious Correlation: A Causal Interpretation," *Journal of the American Statistical Association* 49 [1954] : 467-79; Blalock, "Correlation and Causality: The Multivariate Case," *Social Forces* 39 [1961] : 246-51), even though their "causal models" did not initially make use of the regression foundations of Wright's technique. A large literature has developed since the mid-1960s. For the basics of the technique, see Raymond Boudon, "A Method of Linear Causal Analysis: Dependence Analysis," *American Sociological Review* 30 (1965): 365-74; Otis Dudley Duncan, "Path Analysis: Sociological Examples," *American Journal of Sociology* 72 (1966): 1-16; and D. R. Heise, "Problems in Path Analysis and Causal Inference," in *Sociological Methodology 1969*, ed. E. F. Borgatta and George W. Bohrnstedt (San Francisco: Jossey-Bass, 1969), pp. 38-73.

The question remains whether regression analysis should be used at all for a set of variables that include so many measured at the ordinal level. The decision to do so appears to be justified by a number of findings about the effects of violating the assumptions of parametric statistics. See especially C. H. Boneau, "The Effects of Violations of Assumptions Underlying the *t* Test," *Psychological Bulletin* 57 (1960): 49-64; E. F. Borgatta, "My Student the Purist: A Lament," *Sociological Quarterly* 9 (1968): 29-34; and, for an excellent overview of work on this topic, George W. Bohrnstedt and T. Michael Carter, "Robustness in Regression Analysis," in *Sociological Methodology 1971*, ed. Herbert Costner (San Francisco: Jossey-Bass, 1971), pp. 118-46. For this study, the main source of error probably stems from measurement error rather than the regression use of ordinal data.

7. For explanations of the two-stage least-squares technique (or the Thiel-Bassman method, after its two progenitors), see Ronald J. Wonnacott and Thomas H. Wonnacott, *Econometrics* (New York: John Wiley and Sons, 1970), chaps. 17, 19, and 20; and J. Johnston, *Econometrics Methods* (New York: McGraw-Hill, 1963), pp. 258-60. For sample applications see Robert Mason and Albert N. Halter, "The Application of Simultaneous Equations to an Innovation Diffusion Model," in *Causal Models in the Social Sciences*, ed. H. M. Blalock, Jr. (Chicago: Aldine, 1971), pp. 200-218 and 219-24, respectively. The most elaborate application to date is Douglas A. Hibbs, Jr., *Mass Political Violence: A Cross-National Causal Analysis* (New York: John Wiley and Sons, 1973). See especially Appendix 3 of Hibbs's book for a (relatively) clear mathematical motivation of the technique.

8. Taken from Duncan, "Path Analysis," op. cit., pp. 5-6.

Table B.1
Correlation Matrix of the Quantified Variables

NOTE: Decimal points are omitted.
*Item-index correlations corrected for part-whole spuriousness.

	01	02	03	04	05	06	07	08	09	10	11	12	13	14	15	16	17	18	19	20	21	22	23	24	25	26	PI	CI
1. Accessibility	—																											
2. Cultivation of cash crops	22	—																										
3. Temple upkeep	-11	-04	—																									
4. Membership in credit coop.	39	20	21	—																								
5. Non-crop leadership income	15	43	-03	21	—																							
6. Percent of leaders in nonagricultural jobs	35	31	32	66	32	—																						
7. Age of village leaders	10	-06	07	-10	13	31	—																					
8. Village leadership experience	22	-26	22	16	07	-06	26	—																				
9. Training programs	-14	-15	-18	-28	19	-12	-02	45	—																			
10. Street upkeep	-14	-26	44	-34	16	19	-12	24	17	—																		
11. Social infrastructure	07	34	-04	21	-18	18	04	19	-09	18	—																	
12. Intra-village economic disparity	42	56	53	57	-01	26	18	14	-11	12	42	—																
13. Upkeep of house compounds	-15	06	15	13	25	05	08	06	22	07	-15	38	—															
14. Magnitude of economic gap between leaders and village	02	07	07	08	07	04	-06	05	-15	14	04	15	15	—														
15. Percent of leaders in a landholding elite	11	14	06	26	06	-12	-39	15	-28	24	24	15	-45	13	—													
16. Government CD inputs	06	06	05	13	24	36	06	02	24	40	40	02	10	11	60	—												
17. Store ownership	-11	25	15	34	15	11	05	36	10	09	25	40	18	20	-18	-18	—											
18. Rice mill ownership	22	33	20	54	20	35	31	13	-18	12	28	28	18	20	18	18	-03	—										
19. Commercial vehicle ownership	40	25	-02	18	18	14	04	20	01	11	26	01	-05	01	07	07	41	29	—									
20. Nonagricultural employment	40	17	-07	25	-07	42	21	27	31	-04	15	-27	-04	-19	32	35	19	52	56	—								
21. Village-initiated development projects	-04	17	18	22	03	15	15	06	12	14	35	02	09	-10	02	45	19	04	17	02	—							
22. Evidence of low-income group demoralization	19	01	-39	08	-39	11	01	-28	-26	30	12	18	-64	-05	-02	02	-01	33	18	28	-10	—						
23. Level of substandard housing	15	-16	-34	-19	-34	-11	-11	-25	-16	-13	-04	-04	-33	24	40	-21	-18	-27	16	-46	-19	-10	—					
24. Level of superior housing	34	36	02	35	03	20	20	06	11	20	25	42	24	-04	-09	12	19	61	35	46	-03	22	-46	—				
25. Land and water resources	05	42	24	18	24	06	06	36	-34	05	16	77	04	30	20	-01	11	10	11	06	01	11	35	-25	20	—		
26. Economic infrastructure	34	52	42	27	42	29	29	-12	05	27	21	53	26	20	-10	14	-04	35	29	03	-03	00	24	53	34	—		
Personal Investment Index	38	10*	-03	21*	52	42	10	05	11	-25	42	57	15	12	05	15	25*	25*	38*	46*	15	24	-36	26	62	44	—	
Civic Investment Index	-16	-02	41*	00	03	17	06	40	37	47*	00	-04	32*	-23	-32	35	07	-08	01	07	20*	-61	-45	10	-11	-01	02	—

BIBLIOGRAPHY

Apter, David E. *The Politics of Modernization*. Chicago: University of Chicago Press, 1965.

Arensberg, Conrad M., and Arthur H. Niehoff. *Introducing Social Change: A Manual for Americans Overseas*. Chicago: Aldine, 1964.

Armer, Michael. "Formal Education and Psychological Malaise in an African Society." *Sociology of Education* 43 (1970): 143-58.

——, and Allan Schainberg. "Measuring Individual Modernity: A Near Myth." *American Sociological Review* 37 (1972): 301-16.

Banfield, Edward C. *The Moral Basis of a Backward Society*. Glencoe, Ill.: Free Press, 1958.

Binder, Leonard. "Crises in Political Development." in *Crises and Sequences in Political Development*, edited by Binder et al. Princeton, N.J.: Princeton University Press, 1971.

Blalock, H. M., Jr. "Correlation and Causality: The Multivariate Case." *Social Forces* 39 (1961): 246-51.

Bohrnstedt, George W., and T. Michael Carter. "Robustness in Regression Analysis." In *Sociological Methodology 1971*, edited by Herbert Costner. San Francisco: Jossey-Bass, 1971.

Boneau, C. H. "The Effects of Violations of Assumptions Underlying the *t* Test." *Psychological Bulletin* 57 (1960): 49-64.

Borgatta, E. F. "My Student, the Purist: A Lament." *Sociological Quarterly* 9 (1968): 29-34.

Boudon, Raymond. "A Method of Linear Causal Analysis: Dependence Analysis." *American Sociological Review* 30 (1965): 365-74.

Brewster, John M. "Traditional Social Structures as Barriers to Change." In *Agricultural Development and Economic Growth*, edited by Herman M. Southworth and Bruce F. Johnston. Ithaca, N.Y.: Cornell University Press.

Cronbach, L. J. "Coefficient *Alpha* and the Internal Structure of Tests." *Psychometrika* 16 (1951): 297-334.

Deutsch, Karl W. *Nationalism and Social Communication: An Inquiry into the Foundations of Nationality*. Cambridge: MIT Press, 1953.

130

———. "Social Mobilization and Political Development." *American Political Science Review* 55 (1961): 493–514.

Dube, S. C. *Indian Village*. Ithaca, N.Y.: Cornell University Press, 1955.

Duncan, Otis Dudley. "Path Analysis: Sociological Examples." *American Journal of Sociology* 72 (1966): 1–16.

———. "Peer Influences on Aspirations." In *Causal Models in the Social Sciences*, edited by H. M. Blalock, Jr. Chicago: Aldine, 1971, pp. 219–44.

Embree, John F. "Thailand: A Loosely Structured Social System." *American Anthropologist* 52 (1950): 101–93.

Evers, Hans-Dieter, ed. *Loosely Structured Social Systems: Thailand in Comparative Perspective*. New Haven, Conn.: Yale Southeast Asia Studies, 1969.

Flanagan, John C. "The Critical Incident Technique." *Psychological Bulletin* 51 (1954): 327–58.

Foster, George M. "Peasant Society and the Image of Limited Good." *American Anthropologist* 67 (1965): 293–315.

Frey, Frederick W. "Developmental Aspects of Administration." In *Behavioral Change in Agriculture*, edited by J. Paul Leagans and Charles P. Loomis. Ithaca, N.Y.: Cornell University Press, 1971.

Geertz, Clifford. "The Rotating Credit Association: A 'Middle Rung' in Development." *Economic Development and Cultural Change* 10 (1962): 241–63.

Hagen, Everett E. "How Economic Growth Begins: A Theory of Social Change." *Journal of Social Issues* 19 (1963): 20–34.

Heise, D. R. "Problems in Path Analysis and Causal Inference." In *Sociological Methodology 1969*, edited by E. F. Borgatta and George W. Bohrnstedt. San Francisco: Jossey-Bass, 1969, pp. 38–73.

Hibbs, Douglas A., Jr. *Mass Political Violence: A Cross-National Causal Analysis*. New York: John Wiley and Sons, 1973.

Huntington, Samuel P. *Political Order in Changing Societies* New Haven, Conn.: Yale University Press, 1968.

Ingram, James C. *Economic Change in Thailand Since 1850*. Stanford: Stanford University Press, 1955.

Kahl, Joseph A. *The Measurement of Modernism*. Austin: University of Texas Press, 1968.

Kaufman, Howard K. *Bangkhuad: A Community Study in Thailand*. New York: J. J. Augustin, 1960.

Kelley, Truman Lee. *Fundamentals of Statistics*. Cambridge: Harvard University Press, 1947.

Krug, Robert E. *Some Evaluations of ARD Impact in Four Amphoe*. Bangkok: American Institutes for Research, 1972.

———, and Steven M. Jung. *Systems for Evaluating the Impact of Rural Development Programs*. Bangkok: American Institutes for Research, 1974.

Krug, Robert E., Paul A. Schwarz, and Suchitra Bhakdi. "Measuring Village Commitment to Development." In *Values in Development: Appraising Asian Experience*, edited by Harold Lasswell, Daniel Lerner, and John D. Montgomery. Cambridge: MIT Press, 1976, pp. 104–132.

Le May, Reginal S. *An Asian Arcady: The Land and People of Northern Siam*. London: Cambridge University Press, 1926.

Lerner, Daniel. *The Passing of Traditional Society: Modernizing the Middle East*. New York: Free Press, 1958.

Lewis, Oscar. *Life in a Mexican Village: Tepoztlan Restudied*. Urbana: University of Illinois Press, 1951.

Lopreato, Joseph. "Interpersonal Relations in Peasant Society: The Peasant's View." *Human Organization* 21 (1962): 21-24.

McClelland, David C. *The Achieving Society*. Princeton, N.J.: Van Nostrand, 1961.

———, J. W. Atkinson, R. A. Clark, and E. L. Lowell. *The Achievement Motive*. New York: Appleton-Century-Crofts, 1953.

Mason, Robert, and Albert N. Halter. "The Application of Simultaneous Equations to an Innovation Diffusion Model." In *Causal Models in the Social Sciences*, edited by H. M. Blalock, Jr. Chicago: Aldine, 1971, pp. 200-218.

Marzouk, G. A. *Economic Development and Policies: Case Study of Thailand*. Rotterdam: Rotterdam University Press, 1972.

Mead, Margaret, ed. *Cultural Patterns and Technical Change*. New York: Mentor, 1955.

Merton, Robert K., and Patricial L. Kendall. "The Focused Interview." *American Journal of Sociology* 51 (1946): 541-57.

Moerman, Michael. *Agricultural Change and Peasant Choice in a Thai Village*. Berkeley and Los Angeles: University of California Press, 1968.

———. "A Thai Village Headman as a Synaptic Leader." *Journal of Asian Studies* (May 1969): 535-49.

Montgomery, John D. *Technology and Civic Life: Making and Implementing Development Decisions*. Cambridge: MIT Press, 1974.

Mosel, James N. "Communications Patterns and Political Socialization in Transitional Thailand." In *Communications and Political Development*, edited by Lucian W. Pye. Princeton, N.J.: Princeton University Press, 1963, pp. 184-228.

Murray, Charles A. *Thai Local Administration: Villager Interactions with Community and Amphoe Administration*. Bangkok: USAID, 1968.

———. *Village Level Disposing Conditions for Development Impact*. Bangkok: American Institutes for Research, 1968.

National FAO Committee on Thailand. *Thailand and Her Agricultural Problems*. Bangkok: Thai Ministry of Agriculture, 1949.

Niehoff, Arthur H. *A Casebook of Social Change*. Chicago: Aldine Press, 1966.

Quint, Malcolm. "The Idea of Progress in an Iraqi Village." *Middle East Journal* 12 (1958): 369–84.

Phillips, Herbert P. *Thai Peasant Personality: The Patterning of Interpersonal Behavior in the Village of Bang Chan*. Berkeley and Los Angeles: University of California Press, 1965.

Reichel-Dolmatoff, Gerardo, and Alicia Reichel-Dolmatoff. *The People of Aritama*. Chicago: University of Chicago Press, 1961.

Rogers, Everett M., and Lynne Svenning. *Modernization Among Peasants: The Impact of Communication*. New York: Holt, Rinehart and Winston, 1969.

Rubin, Herbert J., and Irene S. Rubin. "Effects of Institutional Change upon a Dependency Culture: The Commune Council 275 in Rural Thailand." *Asian Survey* 13 (1973): 270–87.

Schnaiberg, Allan. "Rural-Urban Residence and Modernism: A Study of Ankara Province, Turkey." *Demography* 7 (1970): 71–85.

Sharp, Lauriston, Hazel M. Hauck, Kamol Janlekha, and Robert B. Textor. *Siamese Rice Village: A Preliminary Study of Bang Chan 1948–1949*. Bangkok: Cornell Research Center, 1953.

Simon, Herbert A. "Spurious Correlation: A Causal Interpretation." *Journal of the American Statistical Association* 49 (1954): 467–79.

Smith, David H., and Alex Inkeles. "The OM Scale: A Comparative Socio-Psychological Measure of Individual Modernity." *Sociometry* 29 (1966): 353–77.

Spicer, H. H., ed. *Human Problems in Technical Change*. New York: Russell Sage Foundation, 1952.

United Nations. Department of Economic and Social Affairs. *Yearbook of National Accounts Statistics 1972*, vol. 2. New York: United Nations, 1973.

Wonnacott, Ronald J., and Thomas H. Wonnacott. *Econometrics*. New York: John Wiley and Sons, 1970.

Wright, Seward. "Correlation and Causation." *Journal of Agricultural Research* 20 (1921): 557–85.

Zimmerman, Carl C. *Siam: Rural Economic Survey, 1930–1931*. Bangkok: Bangkok Times Press, 1931.

ABOUT THE AUTHOR

CHARLES A. MURRAY is a Principal Research Scientist at the American Institutes for Research in the Behavioral Sciences in Washington, D.C. His field of specialization is the development of methods for evaluating social action programs.

During six years in Thailand, Dr. Murray first served for two years as a Peace Corps Volunteer in the Thai government's Village Health Program. He then moved on to a series of village-based research efforts that culminated in the work that led to this book. During this period, Dr. Murray participated in studies conducted for the Agency for Accelerated Rural Development, the Community Development Department, the Provincial Police, and the Department of Local Administration.

Dr. Murray holds a B.A. in history from Harvard University and a Ph.D. in Political Science from the Massachusetts Institute of Technology.

AGRICULTURAL SUPPLY RESPONSE: A Survey of the
Econometric Evidence
                        Hossein Askari
                        John Thomas Cumings

AGRICULTURE IN THE PEOPLE'S REPUBLIC OF CHINA:
Structural Changes and Technical Transformation
                        Leslie T. Kuo

*DEVELOPMENT WITHOUT DEPENDENCE
                        Pierre Uri

ORGANIZATION FOR RURAL DEVELOPMENT: Risk Taking
and Appropriate Technology
                        Allen Jedlicka

RURAL COMMUNITIES: Inter-Cooperation and Development
                        edited by Yehuda H. Landau
                        Maurice Konopnicki
                        Henri Desroche
                        Placide Rambaud

*Also available in paperback as a PSS Student Edition.